LACY AFGHANS

Ready for a crochet adventure that will result in a luscious home accessory? Choose any of these eight impressive lace afghans.

LEISURE ARTS, INC. • Maumelle, Arkansas

SHELL GALLERY

Finished Size: 46" x 61"
(117 cm x 155 cm)

INTERMEDIATE

SHOPPING LIST

Yarn (Medium Weight) [4 MEDIUM]
[6 ounces, 315 yards
(170.1 grams, 288 meters) per skein]:

- ☐ 8 skeins

Crochet Hook

- ☐ Size I (5.5 mm)
  or size needed for gauge

GAUGE INFORMATION

13 dc and 7 rows = 4" (10 cm)
Gauge Swatch: 4" (10 cm) square
Ch 15.
Row 1: Dc in fourth ch from hook **(3 skipped chs count as first dc)** and in each ch across: 13 dc.
Rows 2-7: Ch 2 **(counts as first dc)**, turn; dc in next dc and in each dc across.
Finish off.

STITCH GUIDE

FRONT POST TRIPLE TREBLE CROCHET ***(abbreviated FPtrtr)***
YO 4 times, insert hook from **front** to **back** around post of st indicated ***(Fig. 3, page 47)***, YO and pull up a loop (6 loops on hook), (YO and draw through 2 loops on hook) 5 times.

BACK POST TRIPLE TREBLE CROCHET ***(abbreviated BPtrtr)***
YO 4 times, insert hook from **back** to **front** around post of st indicated ***(Fig. 3, page 47)***, YO and pull up a loop (6 loops on hook), (YO and draw through 2 loops on hook) 5 times.

2-DC CLUSTER (uses one sp)
★ YO, insert hook in sp indicated, YO and pull up a loop, YO and draw through 2 loops on hook; repeat from ★ once **more**, YO and draw through all 3 loops on hook.

4-DC CLUSTER (uses one dc)
★ YO, insert hook in dc indicated, YO and pull up a loop, YO and draw through 2 loops on hook; repeat from ★ 3 times **more**, YO and draw through all 5 loops on hook.

RIGHT FP CLUSTER
First Leg: YO 4 times, insert hook from **front** to **back** around post of st 2 rows **below** ***(Fig. 3, page 47)*** **or** around post of Second Leg on previous Right FP Cluster (working **before** previous Cluster), YO and pull a loop (6 loops on hook), (YO and draw through 2 loops on hook) 4 times (2 loops remaining on hook).
Second Leg: YO, working **behind** First Leg, insert hook in next dc, YO and pull up a loop (4 loops on hook), YO and draw through 2 loops on hook, YO and draw through all 3 loops on hook.

LEFT FP CLUSTER
First Leg: YO, insert hook in next st, YO and pull up a loop, YO and draw through 2 loops on hook (2 loops remaining on hook).
Second Leg: YO 4 times, insert hook from **front** to **back** around post of st 2 rows **below** same st ***(Fig. 3, page 47)*** **or** around post of First Leg on previous Left FP Cluster (working **after** previous Cluster), YO and pull up a loop (7 loops on hook), (YO and draw through 2 loops on hook) 4 times, YO and draw through all 3 loops on hook.

AFGHAN

Ch 153.

Row 1 (Right side)**:** Dc in fourth ch from hook **(3 skipped chs count as first dc)** and in each ch across: 151 dc.

Note: Loop a short piece of yarn around any stitch to mark Row 1 as **right** side.

Row 2: Ch 2 **(counts as first dc, now and throughout)**, turn; dc in next 4 dc, ★ † ch 3, skip next 2 dc, sc in next dc, ch 4, skip next dc, sc in next dc, ch 3, skip next 2 dc, dc in next 5 dc, ch 5, skip next 5 dc, sc in next dc, ch 4, skip next dc, sc in next dc, ch 5, skip next 5 dc, dc in next 5 dc, ch 3, skip next 2 dc, sc in next dc, ch 4, skip next dc, sc in next dc, ch 3, skip next 2 dc, dc in next 5 dc †, ch 2, skip next 2 dc, dc in next dc, ch 2, skip next 2 dc, dc in next 5 dc; repeat from ★ once **more**, then repeat from † to † once: 80 sts and 31 sps.

Row 3: Ch 2, turn; ★ † dc in next 3 dc, work Right FP Cluster, ch 1, skip next ch-3 sp, work 2-dc Cluster in next ch-4 sp, (ch 3, work 2-dc Cluster in same sp) twice, ch 1, skip next ch-3 sp, work Left FP Cluster, dc in next 3 dc, work Right FP Cluster, ch 3, sc in next ch-5 sp, ch 1, 7 dc in next ch-4 sp, ch 1, sc in next ch-5 sp, ch 3, work Left FP Cluster, dc in next 3 dc, work Right FP Cluster, ch 1, skip next ch-3 sp, work 2-dc Cluster in next ch-4 sp, (ch 3, work 2-dc Cluster in same sp) twice, ch 1, skip next ch-3 sp, work Left FP Cluster, dc in next 3 dc †, work Right FP Cluster, ch 1, skip next ch-2 sp, (2 dc, ch 1) twice in next dc, skip next ch-2 sp, work Left FP Cluster; repeat from ★ once **more**, then repeat from † to † once, skip last st, work FPtrtr around next-to-last st 2 rows **below**: 113 sts and 42 sps.

Row 4: Ch 2, turn; dc in next 4 sts, ★ † ch 3, skip next ch-1 sp, sc in next ch-3 sp, ch 4, sc in next ch-3 sp, ch 3, skip next 2-dc Cluster and next ch-1 sp, dc in next 5 sts, ch 2, skip next 2 sps, work 4-dc Cluster in next dc, (ch 3, skip next dc, work 4-dc Cluster in next dc) 3 times, ch 2, skip next 2 sps, dc in next 5 sts, ch 3, skip next ch-1 sp, sc in next ch-3 sp, ch 4, sc in next ch-3 sp, ch 3, skip next 2-dc Cluster and next ch-1 sp †, dc in next 5 sts, ch 2, skip next ch-1 sp, dc in next ch-1 sp, ch 2, skip next 2 dc, dc in next 5 sts; repeat from ★ once **more**, then repeat from † to † once, dc in next 4 sts, skip last st, work BPtrtr around next-to-last st 2 rows **below**: 86 sts and 37 sps.

Row 5: Ch 2, turn; dc in next 3 dc, ★ † work Right FP Cluster, ch 1, skip next ch-3 sp, work 2-dc Cluster in next ch-4 sp, (ch 3, work 2-dc Cluster in same sp) twice, ch 1, skip next ch-3 sp, work Left FP Cluster, dc in next 3 dc, work Right FP Cluster, ch 3, skip next ch-2 sp, sc in next ch-3 sp, (ch 4, sc in next ch-3 sp) twice, ch 3, skip next ch-2 sp, work Left FP Cluster, dc in next 3 dc, work Right FP Cluster, ch 1, skip next ch-3 sp, work 2-dc Cluster in next ch-4 sp, (ch 3, work 2-dc Cluster in same sp) twice, ch 1, skip next ch-3 sp, work Left FP Cluster, dc in next 3 dc †, work Right FP Cluster, ch 1, skip next ch-2 sp, (2 dc, ch 1) twice in next dc, skip next ch-2 sp, work Left FP Cluster, dc in next 3 dc; repeat from ★ once **more**, then repeat from † to † once, skip last st, work FPtrtr around next-to-last st 2 rows **below**: 95 sts and 42 sps.

Row 6: Ch 2, turn; dc in next 4 sts, ★ † ch 3, skip next ch-1 sp, sc in next ch-3 sp, ch 4, sc in next ch-3 sp, ch 3, skip next 2-dc Cluster and next ch-1 sp, dc in next 5 sts, ch 5, skip next ch-3 sp, sc in next ch-4 sp, ch 4, sc in next ch-4 sp, ch 5, skip next ch-3 sp, dc in next 5 sts, ch 3, skip next ch-1 sp, sc in next ch-3 sp, ch 4, sc in next ch-3 sp, ch 3, skip next 2-dc Cluster and next ch-1 sp †, dc in next 5 sts, ch 2, skip next ch-1 sp, dc in next ch-1 sp, ch 2, skip next 2 dc, dc in next 5 sts; repeat from ★ once **more**, then repeat from † to † once, dc in next 4 sts, skip last st, work BPtrtr around next-to-last st 2 rows **below**: 80 sts and 31 sps.

Rows 7-107: Repeat Rows 3-6, 25 times; then repeat Row 3 once **more**.

Finish off.

FRINGE

Using photo as a guide for placement and holding 8 strands of yarn together, each 14" (35.5 cm) long, add 21 fringe groups evenly spaced across each short edge of Afghan *(Figs. 6a & b, page 47)*.

TRIANGLES

Finished Size: 42" x 64"
(106.5 cm x 162.5 cm)

INTERMEDIATE

SHOPPING LIST

Yarn (Medium Weight) 4
[3.5 ounces, 205 yards
(100 grams,187 meters) per skein]:
☐ 13 skeins

Crochet Hook
☐ Size I (5.5 mm)
or size needed for gauge

GAUGE INFORMATION

13 dc and 7 rows = 4" (10 cm)
Gauge Swatch: 4" (10 cm) square
Ch 16.
Row 1: Dc in fourth ch from hook **(3 skipped chs count as first dc)** and in each ch across: 13 dc.
Rows 2-7: Ch 2 **(counts as first dc)**, turn; dc in next dc and in each dc across.
Finish off.

STITCH GUIDE

TREBLE CROCHET ***(abbreviated tr)***
YO twice, insert hook in st indicated, YO and pull up a loop (4 loops on hook), (YO and draw through 2 loops on hook) 3 times.

FRONT POST TREBLE CROCHET ***(abbreviated FPtr)***
YO twice, insert hook from **front** to **back** around post of st indicated ***(Fig. 3, page 47)***, YO and pull up a loop (4 loops on hook), (YO and draw through 2 loops on hook) 3 times.

BACK POST TREBLE CROCHET ***(abbreviated BPtr)***
YO twice, insert hook from **back** to **front** around post of st indicated ***(Fig. 3, page 47)***, YO and pull up a loop (4 loops on hook), (YO and draw through 2 loops on hook) 3 times.

FRONT POST TRIPLE TREBLE CROCHET ***(abbreviated FPtrtr)***
YO 4 times, insert hook from **front** to **back** around post of st indicated ***(Fig. 3, page 47)***, YO and pull up a loop (6 loops on hook), (YO and draw through 2 loops on hook) 5 times.

BACK POST TRIPLE TREBLE CROCHET ***(abbreviated BPtrtr)***
YO 4 times, insert hook from **back** to **front** around post of st indicated ***(Fig. 3, page 47)***, YO and pull up a loop (6 loops on hook), (YO and draw through 2 loops on hook) 5 times.

FRONT POST 2 TOGETHER ***(abbreviated FP2tog)*** (uses next 3 sts)
YO twice, insert hook from **front** to **back** around post of same BPtr just worked into ***(Fig. 3, page 47)***, † YO and pull up a loop, (YO and draw through 2 loops on hook) twice †, YO twice, skip next dc, insert hook from **front** to **back** around next BPtr, repeat from † to † once, YO and draw through all 3 loops on hook **(counts as one st)**.

RIGHT FP CLUSTER
First Leg: YO 4 times, insert hook from **front** to **back** around post of st 2 rows **below** ***(Fig. 3, page 47)*** **or** around post of Second Leg on previous Right FP Cluster (working **after** previous Right FP Cluster), YO and pull up a loop (6 loops on hook), (YO and draw through 2 loops on hook) 4 times (2 loops remaining on hook).
Second Leg: YO, working **behind** First Leg, insert hook in next st, YO and pull up a loop (4 loops on hook), YO and draw through 2 loops on hook, YO and draw through all 3 loops on hook.

LEFT FP CLUSTER
First Leg: YO, insert hook in next st, YO and pull up a loop, YO and draw through 2 loops on hook (2 loops remaining on hook).
Second Leg: YO 4 times, insert hook from **front** to **back** around post of st 2 rows **below** same st ***(Fig. 3, page 47)*** **or** around post of First Leg on previous Left FP Cluster (working **before** previous left FP Cluster), YO and pull up a loop (7 loops on hook), (YO and draw through 2 loops on hook) 4 times, YO and draw through all 3 loops on hook.

AFGHAN

Ch 137.

Row 1 (Right side)**:** Dc in fourth ch from hook **(3 skipped chs count as first dc)** and in each ch across: 135 dc.

Note: Loop a short piece of yarn around any stitch to mark Row 1 as **right** side.

Row 2: Ch 2 **(counts as first dc, now and throughout)**, turn; dc in Front Loop Only of next 24 dc ***(Fig. 1, page 46)***, skip next dc, (dc, ch 1, dc) in **both** loops of next dc, skip next dc, ★ dc in Front Loop Only of next 38 dc, skip next dc, (dc, ch 1, dc) in **both** loops of next dc, skip next dc; repeat from ★ once **more**, dc in Front Loop Only of last 25 dc: 132 dc and 3 ch-1 sps.

Row 3: Ch 2, turn; dc in Back Loop Only of next 4 dc ***(Fig. 1, page 46)***, work Right FP Cluster, work Left FP Cluster, dc in Back Loop Only of next 4 dc, ★ † ch 1, skip next 3 dc, (3 dc, ch 1) twice in **both** loops of next dc, skip next 3 dc †, dc in Back Loop Only of next 6 dc, skip next dc, work FPtr around next dc, ch 1, (dc, ch 1) twice in next ch-1 sp, work FPtr around next dc, skip next dc, dc in Back Loop Only of next 6 dc, repeat from † to † once, dc in Back Loop Only of next 4 dc, work Right FP Cluster, work Left FP Cluster, dc in Back Loop Only of next 4 dc; repeat from ★ 2 times **more**, skip last dc, work FPtrtr around next-to-last dc 2 rows **below**: 126 sts and 27 ch-1 sps.

Row 4: Ch 2, turn; dc in Front Loop Only of next 10 sts, ★ † work BPtr around same dc just worked into, ch 1, skip next 3 dc, (2 dc, ch 1) twice in next ch-1 sp, skip next 3 dc, work BPtr around next dc †, dc in Front Loop Only of same dc just worked around and next 4 dc, skip next dc, work BPtr around next FPtr, ch 1, skip next ch-1 sp, (2 dc, ch 1) twice in next ch-1 sp, skip next dc, work BPtr around next FPtr, skip next dc, dc in Front Loop Only of next 5 dc, repeat from † to † once, dc in Front Loop Only of same dc just worked around and next 9 sts; repeat from ★ 2 times **more**, skip last dc, work BPtrtr around next-to-last dc two rows **below**.

Row 5: Ch 2, turn; dc in Back Loop Only of next 4 dc, work Right FP Cluster, work Left FP Cluster, ★ † dc in Back Loop Only of next 5 sts, work FPtr around same BPtr just worked into, ch 1, skip next ch-1 sp, (dc, ch 1) twice in next ch-1 sp, skip next 2 dc, work FPtr around next BPtr, dc in Back Loop Only of same BPtr just worked around and next 4 dc †, skip next dc, work FPtr around next BPtr, ch 1, skip next ch-1 sp, (3 dc, ch 1) twice in next ch-1 sp, skip next 2 dc, work FPtr around next BPtr, skip next dc, repeat from † to † once, work (Right FP Cluster, Left FP Cluster); repeat from ★ 2 times **more**, dc in Back Loop Only of next 4 dc, skip last dc, work FPtrtr around next-to-last dc 2 rows **below**.

Row 6: Ch 2, turn; dc in Front Loop Only of next 12 sts, ★ † work BPtr around same FPtr just worked into, ch 1, skip next ch-1 sp, dc in next ch-1 sp, ch 1, skip next ch-1 sp, work BPtr around next FPtr, dc in Front Loop Only of same FPtr just worked around and next 4 dc, skip next dc, work BPtr around next FPtr, ch 1, skip next ch-1 sp, (4 dc, ch 1) twice in next ch-1 sp, skip next 3 dc, work BPtr around next FPtr, skip next dc, dc in Front Loop Only of next 5 sts, work BPtr around same FPtr just worked into, ch 1, skip next ch-1 sp, dc in next ch-1 sp, ch 1, skip next ch-1 sp, work BPtr around next FPtr †, dc in Front Loop Only of same FPtr just worked around and next 13 sts; repeat from ★ once **more**, then repeat from † to † once, dc in Front Loop Only of same FPtr just worked around and next 11 sts, skip last dc, work BPtrtr around next-to-last dc two rows **below**: 132 sts and 21 ch-1 sps.

Row 7: Ch 2, turn; dc in Back Loop Only of next 4 dc, work Right FP Cluster, work Left FP Cluster, ★ dc in Back Loop Only of next 7 sts, work FP2tog, dc in Back Loop Only of same BPtr just worked around and next 4 dc, skip next dc, work FPtr around next BPtr, ch 1, skip next ch-1 sp, work (tr, 7 dc, tr) in next ch-1 sp, ch 1, skip next 4 dc, work FPtr around next

BPtr, skip next dc, dc in Back Loop Only of next 5 sts, work FP2tog, dc in Back Loop Only of same BPtr just worked around and next 6 dc, work Right FP Cluster, Left FP Cluster; repeat from ★ 2 times **more**, dc in Back Loop Only of next 4 dc, skip last dc, work FPtrtr around next-to-last dc 2 rows **below**: 129 sts and 6 ch-1 sps.

Row 8: Ch 2, turn; dc in Front Loop Only of next 20 sts, ★ † dc in top loop of next ch, ch 3, skip next 4 sts, (sc, ch 1, sc) in **both** loops of next dc, ch 3, skip next 4 sts, dc in top loop of next ch †, dc in Front Loop Only of next 30 sts; repeat from ★ once **more**, then repeat from † to † once, dc in Front Loop Only of next 20 sts, skip last dc, work BPtrtr around next-to-last dc two rows **below**: 114 sts and 9 sps.

Row 9: Ch 2, turn; dc in Back Loop Only of next 4 dc, work Right FP Cluster, work Left FP Cluster, dc in Back Loop Only of next 4 dc, ★ † ch 1, skip next 3 dc, (3 dc, ch 1) twice in **both** loops of next dc, skip next 3 dc †, dc in Back Loop Only of next 4 dc, dc in top loop of next 2 chs, work FPtr around next sc, ch 1, (dc, ch 1) twice in next ch-1 sp, work FPtr around next sc, skip next ch, dc in top loop of next 2 chs, dc in Back Loop Only of next 4 dc, repeat from † to † once, dc in Back Loop Only of next 4 dc, work Right FP Cluster, work Left FP Cluster, dc in Back Loop Only of next 4 dc; repeat from ★ 2 times **more**, skip last dc, work FPtrtr around next-to-last dc 2 rows **below**: 126 sts and 27 ch-1 sps.

Rows 10-109: Repeat Rows 4-9, 16 times; then repeat Rows 4-7 once **more**.

Row 110: Ch 2, turn; dc in Front Loop Only of next 20 sts, ★ † dc in top loop of next ch, ch 3, skip next 3 sts, slip st in **both** loops of next 3 dc, ch 3, skip next 3 sts, dc in top loop of next ch †, dc in Front Loop Only of next 30 sts; repeat from ★ once **more**, then repeat from † to † once, dc in Front Loop Only of next 20 sts, skip last dc, work BPtrtr around next-to-last dc two rows **below**: 117 sts and 6 ch-3 sps

Row 111: Ch 2, turn; dc in Back Loop Only of next 4 dc, work Right FP Cluster, work Left FP Cluster, ★ dc in Back Loop Only of next 15 dc, dc in top loop of next ch, hdc in top loop of next 2 chs, sc in **both** loops of next 3 slip sts, hdc in top loop of next 2 chs, dc in top loop of next ch, dc in Back Loop Only of next 15 dc, work Right FP Cluster, work Left FP Cluster; repeat from ★ 2 times **more**, dc in Back Loop Only of next 4 dc, skip last dc, work FPtrtr around next-to-last dc 2 rows **below**; finish off.

FRINGE

Using photo as a guide for placement and holding 10 strands of yarn together, each 14" (35.5 cm) long, add 14 groups of fringe evenly spaced across each short edge of Afghan ***(Figs. 6a & b, page 47)***.

VIGNETTES

Finished Size: 40" x 62½"
(101.5 cm x 159 cm)

INTERMEDIATE

SHOPPING LIST

Yarn (Medium Weight) 4
[3.5 ounces, 210 yards
(100 grams, 192 meters) per skein]:
☐ 12 skeins

Crochet Hook
☐ Size I (5.5 mm)
or size needed for gauge

GAUGE INFORMATION

In pattern,
24 sts = 6¾" (17.25 cm);
8 rows = 4 (10 cm)
13 dc and 7 rows = 4" (10 cm)
Gauge Swatch: 4" (10 cm) square
Ch 15.
Row 1: Dc in fourth ch from hook **(3 skipped chs count as first dc)** and in each ch across: 13 dc.
Rows 2-7: Ch 2 **(counts as first dc)**, turn; dc in next dc and in each dc across.
Finish off.

STITCH GUIDE

FRONT POST TREBLE CROCHET *(abbreviated FPtr)*
YO twice, insert hook from **front** to **back** around post of st indicated *(Fig. 3, page 47)*, YO and pull up a loop (4 loops on hook), (YO and draw through 2 loops on hook) 3 times.

BACK POST TREBLE CROCHET *(abbreviated BPtr)*
YO twice, insert hook from **back** to **front** around post of st indicated *(Fig. 3, page 47)*, YO and pull up a loop (4 loops on hook), (YO and draw through 2 loops on hook) 3 times.

BACK POST HALF DOUBLE CROCHET *(abbreviated BPhdc)*
YO, insert hook from **back** to **front** around post of st indicated *(Fig. 3, page 47)*, YO and pull up a loop (3 loops on hook), YO and draw through all 3 loops on hook.

FP CLUSTER (uses one dc)
YO twice, insert hook from **front** to **back** around post of dc indicated *(Fig. 3, page 47)*, YO and pull up a loop (4 loops on hook), (YO and draw through 2 loops on hook) twice (2 loops remaining on hook), YO, insert hook in **side** of two legs of st just made *(Fig. 4, page 47)*, YO and pull up a loop (4 loops on hook), YO and draw through 2 loops on hook, YO and draw through all 3 loops on hook.

DOUBLE CROCHET 2 TOGETHER *(abbreviated dc2tog)*
(uses 2 ch-3 sps)
★ YO, insert hook in **next** ch-3 sp, YO and pull up a loop, YO and draw through 2 loops on hook; repeat from ★ once **more**, YO and draw through all 3 loops on hook **(counts as one dc)**.

SMALL POPCORN (uses one st)
5 Dc in st indicated, drop loop from hook, insert hook in first dc of 5-dc group, hook dropped loop and draw through st. On **wrong** side rows/rnds, insert hook from **back** to **front** in first dc of 5-dc group and complete in same manner.

LARGE POPCORN
(uses one dc and one ch-6 loop)
3 Dc in next dc, working through next ch-6 loop, dc in same dc, working **behind** same loop, 3 dc in same dc, drop loop from hook, insert hook in first dc of 7-dc group, hook dropped loop and draw through st.

7-DC POPCORN (uses one dc)
7 Dc in dc indicated, drop loop from hook, insert hook in first dc of 7-dc group, hook dropped loop and draw through st.

PATTERNS

PATTERN A (uses 11 sts)

Row 1: Dc in next 3 dc, ch 3, skip next 2 dc, in next dc work (sc, ch 12, sc, ch 6, sc, ch 12, sc), ch 3, skip next 2 dc, dc in next 3 dc: 6 dc, 2 ch-3 sps, and 3 loops.

Row 2: Dc in next 3 dc, ch 3, working in **front** of next 3 loops, dc2tog, ch 3, dc in next 3 dc: 7 dc and 2 ch-3 sps.

Row 3: Dc in next dc, † working through next ch-12 loop and being careful **not** to twist, dc in next dc †, ch 3, skip next dc and next ch-3 sp, work Large Popcorn, ch 4, skip next ch-3 sp and next dc, repeat from † to † once, dc in next dc: 5 sts and 2 sps.

Row 4: Dc in next 2 dc, (hdc, 2 sc) in next ch-4 sp, sc in last ch of same ch-4, skip next Popcorn, (2 sc, hdc) in next ch-3 sp, dc in next 2 dc: 11 sts.

PATTERN B (uses 11 sts)

Row 1: Dc in next 4 dc, ch 1, skip next dc, work FP Cluster around next dc, ch 1, skip next dc, dc in next 4 dc: 9 sts and 2 ch-1 sps.

Row 2: Dc in next 2 dc, skip next 2 dc, work (Small Popcorn, ch 3, Small Popcorn) under top 2 loops of next FP Cluster ***(Fig. A)***, ch 1, skip next 2 dc, dc in next 2 dc: 6 sts and 2 sps.

Fig. A

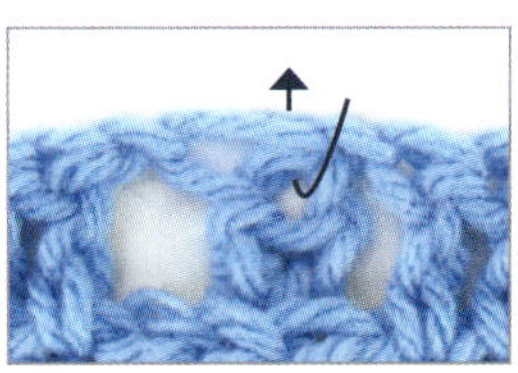

Row 3: Dc in next 2 dc, ch 3, skip next Small Popcorn, work Small Popcorn in center ch of next ch-3, ch 3, skip next Small Popcorn, dc in next 2 dc: 5 sts and 2 ch-3 sps.

Row 4: Dc in next dc, hdc in next dc, (hdc, sc, slip st) in next ch-3 sp, slip st in last ch of same ch-3, skip next Popcorn, (slip st, sc, hdc) in next ch-3 sp, hdc in next dc, dc in next dc: 11 sts.

PATTERN C (uses 11 sts)

Row 1: Dc in next 4 dc, skip next 2 dc, work FPtr around next dc, ch 2, working **behind** FPtr just made, work FPtr around first skipped dc, dc in next 4 dc: 10 sts and one ch-2 sp.

Row 2: Dc in next 3 dc, skip next dc, work BPtr around next FPtr, ch 1, dc in next ch-2 sp, ch 1, work BPtr around next FPtr, skip next dc, dc in next 3 dc: 9 sts and 2 ch-1 sps.

Row 3: Dc in next dc, skip next 2 dc, work FPtr around next BPtr, ch 3, work 7-dc Popcorn in next dc, ch 4, work FPtr around next BPtr, skip next 2 dc, dc in next dc: 5 sts and 2 sps.

Row 4: Dc in next 2 sts, (hdc, 2 sc) in next ch-4 sp, slip st in last ch of same ch-4, skip next Popcorn, (2 sc, hdc) in next ch-3 sp, dc in next 2 sts: 11 sts.

PATTERN D (uses 11 sts)

Row 1: Dc in next 3 dc, ch 1, skip next 2 dc, work (FPtr, ch 3, FPtr) around next dc, skip next 2 dc, dc in next 3 dc: 8 sts and 2 sps.

Row 2: Dc in next 2 dc, skip next dc, work Small Popcorn in next FPtr, ch 3, work Small Popcorn in center ch of next ch-3, ch 3, work Small Popcorn in next FPtr, ch 1, skip next dc, dc in next 2 dc: 7 sts and 3 sps.

Row 3: Dc in next 2 dc, ch 3, skip next Small Popcorn, sc in next ch-3 sp, ch 4, sc in next ch-3 sp, ch 3, skip next Small Popcorn, dc in next 2 dc: 6 sts and 3 sps.

Row 4: Dc in next 2 dc, (hdc, dc) in next ch-3 sp, (dc, hdc, dc) in next ch-4 sp, (dc, hdc) in next ch-3 sp, dc in next 2 dc: 11 sts.

AFGHAN

Ch 136, place marker in second ch from hook for st placement.

Row 1: Sc in second ch from hook and in each ch across: 135 sc.

Row 2 (Right side)**:** Ch 2 **(counts as first dc, now and throughout)**, turn; work FPtr around next sc, working in Back Loops Only ***(Fig. 1, page 46)***, dc in next 11 sc, work FPtr around next sc, ★ ch 1, skip next sc, (dc in next sc, ch 1, skip next sc) 5 times, work FPtr around next sc, dc in next 11 sc, work FPtr around next sc; repeat from ★ across to last sc, dc in last sc.

Note: Loop a short piece of yarn around any stitch to mark Row 2 as **right** side.

Row 3: Ch 2, turn; work BPtr around next FPtr, working in both loops, dc in next 11 dc, work BPtr around next FPtr, ★ dc in next ch-1 sp, (ch 1, dc in next ch-1 sp) 5 times, work BPtr around next FPtr, dc in next 11 dc, work BPtr around next FPtr; repeat from ★ across to last dc, dc in last dc.

Row 4: Ch 2, turn; work FPtr around next BPtr, ♥ Pattern A Row 1, † work FPtr around next BPtr, ch 1, (dc in next ch-1 sp, ch 1) 5 times, work FPtr around next BPtr †, Pattern B Row 1 ♥, repeat from † to † once, Pattern C Row 1, repeat from † to † once, Pattern D Row 1, repeat from † to † once, then repeat from ♥ to ♥ once, work FPtr around next BPtr, dc in last dc.

Row 5: Ch 2, turn; work BPtr around next FPtr, ♥ Pattern B Row 2, † work BPtr around next FPtr, dc in next ch-1 sp, (ch 1, dc in next ch-1 sp) 5 times, work BPtr around next FPtr †, Pattern A Row 2 ♥, repeat from † to † once, Pattern D Row 2, repeat from † to † once, Pattern C Row 2, repeat from † to † once, then repeat from ♥ to ♥ once, work BPtr around next FPtr, dc in last dc.

Row 6: Ch 2, turn; work FPtr around next BPtr, ♥ Pattern A Row 3, † work FPtr around next BPtr, ch 1, (dc in next ch-1 sp, ch 1) 5 times, work FPtr around next BPtr †, Pattern B Row 3 ♥, repeat from † to † once, Pattern C Row 3, repeat from † to † once, Pattern D Row 3, repeat from † to † once, then repeat from ♥ to ♥ once, work FPtr around next BPtr, dc in last dc.

Row 7: Ch 2, turn; work BPtr around next FPtr, ♥ Pattern B Row 4, † work BPtr around next FPtr, dc in next ch-1 sp, (ch 1, dc in next ch-1 sp) 5 times, work BPtr around next FPtr †, Pattern A Row 4 ♥, repeat from † to † once, Pattern D Row 4, repeat from † to † once, Pattern C Row 4, repeat from † to † once, then repeat from ♥ to ♥ once, work BPtr around next FPtr, dc in last dc.

Row 8: Ch 2, turn; work FPtr around next BPtr, dc in next 11 sts, work FPtr around next BPtr, ★ ch 1, (dc in next ch-1 sp, ch 1) 5 times, work FPtr around next BPtr, dc in next 11 sts, work FPtr around next BPtr; repeat from ★ across to last dc, dc in last dc.

Row 9: Ch 2, turn; work BPhdc around next FPtr, ★ sc in Back Loop Only of next 11 sts, work BPhdc around next FPtr; repeat from ★ across to last dc, sc in last dc: 135 sts.

Row 10: Ch 2, turn; work FPtr around next BPhdc; working in free loops of Row 8 ***(Fig. 2a, page 46)***, ch 1, skip next dc, (dc in next dc, ch 1, skip next dc) 5 times, work FPtr around next BPhdc, ★ dc in next 11 sts, work FPtr around next BPhdc, ch 1, skip next dc, (dc in next dc, ch 1, skip next dc) 5 times, work FPtr around next BPhdc; repeat from ★ across to last dc, dc in last dc.

Row 11: Ch 2, turn; work BPtr around next FPtr, dc in next ch-1 sp, (ch 1, dc in next ch-1 sp) 5 times, work BPtr around next FPtr, ★ dc in next 11 dc, work BPtr around next FPtr, dc in next ch-1 sp, (ch 1, dc in next ch-1 sp) 5 times, work BPtr around next FPtr; repeat from ★ across to last dc, dc in last dc.

Row 12: Ch 2, turn; ♥ † work FPtr around next BPtr, ch 1, (dc in next ch-1 sp, ch 1) 5 times, work FPtr around next BPtr **†,** Pattern B Row 1, repeat from † to † once ♥, Pattern C Row 1, repeat from † to † once, Pattern D Row 1, repeat from † to † once, Pattern A Row 1, repeat from ♥ to ♥ once, dc in last dc.

Row 13: Ch 2, turn; ♥ † work BPtr around next FPtr, dc in next ch-1 sp, (ch 1, dc in next ch-1 sp) 5 times, work BPtr around next FPtr †, Pattern B Row 2, repeat from † to † once, Pattern A Row 2, repeat from † to † once ♥, Pattern D Row 2, repeat from † to † once, Pattern C Row 2, repeat from ♥ to ♥ once, dc in last dc.

Row 14: Ch 2, turn; ♥ † work FPtr around next BPtr, ch 1, (dc in next ch-1 sp, ch 1) 5 times, work FPtr around next BPtr **†,** Pattern B Row 3, repeat from † to † once ♥, Pattern C Row 3, repeat from † to † once, Pattern D Row 3, repeat from † to † once, Pattern A Row 3, repeat from ♥ to ♥ once, dc in last dc.

Row 15: Ch 2, turn; ♥ † work BPtr around next FPtr, dc in next ch-1 sp, (ch 1, dc in next ch-1 sp) 5 times, work BPtr around next FPtr †, Pattern B Row 4, repeat from † to † once, Pattern A Row 4, repeat from † to † once ♥, Pattern D Row 4, repeat from † to † once, Pattern C Row 4, repeat from ♥ to ♥ once, dc in last dc.

Row 16: Ch 2, turn; work FPtr around next BPtr, ch 1, (dc in next ch-1 sp, ch 1) 5 times, work FPtr around next BPtr, ★ dc in next 11 sts, work FPtr around next BPtr, ch 1, (dc in next ch-1 sp, ch 1) 5 times, work FPtr around next BPtr; repeat from ★ across to last dc, dc in last dc.

Row 17: Ch 2, turn; work BPhdc around next FPtr, ★ sc in Back Loop Only of next 11 sts, work BPhdc around next FPtr; repeat from ★ across to last dc, sc in last dc: 135 sts.

Row 18: Ch 2, turn; work FPtr around next BPhdc, working in free loops of sts on Row 16, dc in next 11 sts, work FPtr around next BPhdc, ★ ch 1, skip next dc, (dc in next dc, ch 1, skip next dc) 5 times, work FPtr around next BPhdc, dc in next 11 sts, work FPtr around next BPhdc; repeat from ★ across to last dc, dc in last dc.

Rows 19-121: Using Diagram as a guide for Pattern sequence, repeat Rows 3-18, 6 times; then repeat Rows 3-9 once **more**.

Finish off.

DIAGRAM

A		D		C		B		A		D
	D		C		B		A		D	
D		C		B		A		D		C
	C		B		A		D		C	
C		B		A		D		C		B
	B		A		D		C		B	
B		A		D		C		B		A
	A		D		C		B		A	
A		D		C		B		A		D
	D		C		B		A		D	
D		C		B		A		D		C
	C		B		A		D		C	
C		B		A		D		C		B
	B		A		D		C		B	
B		A		D		C		B		A

EDGING

Rnd 1: With **right** side facing and working in sts across Row 121, join yarn with dc in **both** loops of first sc *(see Joining With Dc, page 46)*; dc in Back Loop Only of next BPhdc, ch 1, (skip next st, dc in Back Loop Only of next st, ch 1) across to last 3 sts, skip next sc, dc in next BPhdc, (dc, ch 3, dc) in **both** loops of last sc; ch 1, working in ends of rows, skip first sc row, (dc in next row, ch 1) 7 times, **[**skip next sc row, (dc in next row, ch 1) 7 times**]** across to last sc row; dc in last sc row; working in free loops of beginning ch *(Fig. 2b, page 46)*, (dc, ch 3, dc) in marked ch, remove marker, dc in next ch, ch 1, (skip next ch, dc in next ch, ch 1) across to last 3 chs, skip next ch, dc in next ch, (dc, ch 3, dc) in last ch; working in ends of rows, ch 1, skip first sc row, (dc in next row, ch 1) 7 times, **[**skip next sc row, (dc in next row, ch 1) 7 times**]** across to last row, 2 dc in same st as first dc, ch 3; join with slip st to first dc: 354 dc, 344 ch-1 sps, and 4 corner ch-3 sps.

Rnd 2: Ch 1, **turn**; † sc in next corner ch-3 sp, ch 3, work Small Popcorn in center ch of same ch-3 sp, ch 3, sc in same sp, ch 3 †, skip next dc, work Small Popcorn in next dc, ch 3, skip next ch-1 sp, (sc in next ch-1 sp, ch 3, skip next dc, work Small Popcorn in next dc, ch 3, skip next ch-1 sp) across to next corner ch-3 sp, repeat from † to † once, skip next dc, work Small Popcorn in next dc, ch 3, (skip next ch-1 sp, sc in next ch-1 sp, ch 3, skip next dc, work Small Popcorn in next dc, ch 3) across to next corner ch-3 sp, repeat from † to † once, skip next dc, work Small Popcorn in next dc, ch 3, skip next ch-1 sp, (sc in next ch-1 sp, ch 3, skip next dc, work Small Popcorn in next dc, ch 3, skip next ch-1 sp) across to next corner ch-3 sp, repeat from † to † once, skip next dc, work Small Popcorn in next dc, ch 3, skip next ch-1 sp, (sc in next ch-1 sp, ch 3, skip next dc, work Small Popcorn in next dc, ch 3, skip next ch-1 sp) across; join with slip st to first sc, finish off.

FLORAL CAMEOS

Finished Size: 39" x 56"
(99 cm x 142 cm)

INTERMEDIATE

SHOPPING LIST

Yarn (Medium Weight) MEDIUM 4
[3.5 ounces, 246 yards
(100 grams, 225 meters) per skein**]**:
☐ 8 skeins

Crochet Hook
☐ Size I (5.5 mm)
or size needed for gauge

GAUGE INFORMATION

13 dc and 7 rows = 4" (10 cm)
Gauge Swatch: 4" (10 cm) square
Ch 15.
Row 1: Dc in fourth ch from hook **(3 skipped chs count as first dc)** and in each ch across: 13 dc.
Rows 2-7: Ch 2 **(counts as first dc)**, turn; dc in next dc and in each dc across.
Finish off.

STITCH GUIDE

FRONT POST TREBLE CROCHET *(abbreviated FPtr)*
YO twice, insert hook from **front** to **back** around post of st indicated *(Fig. 3, page 47)*, YO and pull up a loop (4 loops on hook), (YO and draw through 2 loops on hook) 3 times.

BACK POST TREBLE CROCHET *(abbreviated BPtr)*
YO twice, insert hook from **back** to **front** around post of st indicated *(Fig. 3, page 47)*, YO and pull up a loop (4 loops on hook), (YO and draw through 2 loops on hook) 3 times.

FRONT POST DOUBLE TREBLE CROCHET *(abbreviated FPdtr)*
YO 3 times, insert hook from **front** to **back** around post of st indicated *(Fig. 3, page 47)*, YO and pull up a loop (5 loops on hook), (YO and draw through 2 loops on hook) 4 times.

PUFF STITCH *(abbreviated Puff St)* (uses one st or sp)
★ YO, insert hook in st or sp indicated, YO and pull up a loop even with loop on hook; repeat from ★ 2 times **more**, YO and draw through all 7 loops on hook.

3-DC CLUSTER (uses one st or sp)
★ YO, insert hook in st or sp indicated, YO and pull up a loop, YO and draw through 2 loops on hook; repeat from ★ 2 times **more**, YO and draw through all 4 loops on hook.

2-TR CLUSTER (uses one st or sp)
★ YO twice, insert hook in st or sp indicated, YO and pull up a loop, (YO and draw through 2 loops on hook) twice; repeat from ★ once **more**, YO and draw through all 3 loops on hook.

AFGHAN

Ch 129.

Row 1: Dc in fourth ch from hook **(3 skipped chs count as first dc)** and in each ch across to last 2 chs, hdc in next ch, sc in last ch: 127 sts.

Row 2 (Right side)**:** Ch 2 **(counts as first dc, now and throughout)**, turn; dc in next 24 sts, ★ † skip next 2 dc, work FPdtr around next dc, ch 1, working in **front** of FPdtr just made, work FPdtr around first skipped dc †, dc in next 34 dc; repeat from ★ once **more**, then repeat from † to † once, dc in next 24 dc, work FPtr around last dc worked into, leave last dc unworked **(now and throughout)**: 124 sts and 3 ch-1 sps.

Note: Loop a short piece of yarn around any stitch to mark Row 2 as **right** side.

Row 3: Ch 2, turn; dc in next 22 dc, ★ † skip next 2 dc, work BPtr around next FPdtr, ch 1, dc in same FPdtr just worked around, dc in next ch-1 sp and in next FPdtr, ch 1, work BPtr around same FPdtr just worked into, skip next 2 dc †, dc in next 30 dc; repeat from ★ once **more**, then repeat from † to † once, dc in next 22 dc, work BPtr around last dc worked into: 121 sts and 6 ch-1 sps.

Row 4: Ch 2, turn; dc in next 20 dc, ★ † skip next 2 dc, work FPtr around next BPtr, ch 1, dc in same BPtr just worked around, dc in next ch-1 sp and in next 3 dc, dc in next ch-1 sp and in next BPtr, ch 1, work FPtr around same BPtr just worked into, skip next 2 dc †, dc in next 26 dc; repeat from ★ once **more**, then repeat from † to † once, dc in next 20 dc, work FPtr around last dc worked into.

Row 5: Ch 2, turn; dc in next 18 dc, † skip next 2 dc, work BPtr around next FPtr, ch 1, dc in same FPtr just worked around, dc in next ch-1 sp and in next 7 dc, dc in next ch-1 sp and in next FPtr, ch 1, work BPtr around same FPtr just worked into, skip next 2 dc †, dc in next 22 dc, skip next 2 dc, work BPtr around next FPtr, ch 1, dc in same FPtr just worked around, dc in next ch-1 sp and in next 2 dc, ch 1, skip next dc, dc in next dc, ch 1, skip next dc, dc in next 2 dc and in next ch-1 sp, dc in next FPtr, ch 1, work BPtr around FPtr just worked into, skip next 2 dc, dc in next 22 dc, repeat from † to † once, dc in next 18 dc, work BPtr around last dc worked into: 119 sts and 8 ch-1 sps.

Row 6: Ch 2, turn; dc in next 16 dc, † skip next 2 dc, work FPtr around next BPtr, ch 1, dc in same BPtr just worked around, dc in next ch-1 sp and in next 4 dc, ch 1, skip next dc, sc in next dc, ch 1, skip next dc, dc in next 4 dc, dc in next ch-1 sp and in next BPtr, ch 1, work FPtr around same BPtr just worked into, skip next 2 dc †, dc in next 18 dc, skip next 2 dc, work FPtr around next BPtr, ch 1, dc in same BPtr just worked around and in next ch-1 sp, dc in next 2 dc, ch 2, skip next 2 dc, (dc, ch 2, dc) in next dc, ch 2, skip next 2 dc, dc in next 2 dc, dc in next ch-1 sp and in next BPtr, ch 1, work FPtr around same BPtr just worked into, skip next 2 dc, dc in next 18 dc, repeat from † to † once, dc in next 16 dc, work FPtr around last dc worked into: 112 sts and 13 sps.

Row 7: Ch 2, dc in next 15 dc, † skip next dc, work BPtr around next FPtr, ch 1, dc in next ch-1 sp and in next 5 dc, ch 3, skip next dc, sc in next sc, ch 3, skip next dc, dc in next 5 dc and in next ch-1 sp, ch 1, work BPtr around next FPtr, skip next dc †, dc in next 16 dc, skip next dc, work BPtr around next FPtr, ch 1, dc in next ch-1 sp and in next 3 dc, ch 2, skip next ch-2 sp, (work Puff St, ch 2) 3 times in next ch-2 sp, skip next ch-2 sp and next dc, dc in next 3 dc and in next ch-1 sp, ch 1, work BPtr around next FPtr, skip next dc, dc in next 16 dc, repeat from † to † once, dc in next 15 dc, work BPtr around last dc worked into: 107 sts and 14 sps.

Row 8: Ch 2, turn; dc in next 14 dc, † skip next dc, work FPtr around next BPtr, ch 1, dc in next ch-1 sp and in next 5 dc, ch 3, skip next dc and next ch-3 sp, work (3-dc Cluster, ch 3) twice in next sc, skip next ch-3 sp and next dc, dc in next 5 dc and in next ch-1 sp, ch 1, work FPtr around next BPtr, skip next dc †, dc in next 15 dc, work FPtr around next BPtr, ch 1, dc in next 3 dc, ch 4, skip next dc and next ch-2 sp, work (Puff St, ch 2) twice in next ch-2 sp, work (Puff St, ch 2, Puff St) in next ch-2 sp, ch 4, skip next ch-2 sp and next dc, dc in next 3 dc, ch 1, work FPtr around next BPtr, dc in next 15 dc, repeat from † to † once, dc in next 14 dc, work FPtr around last dc worked into: 104 sts and 17 sps.

Row 9: Ch 2, turn; dc in next 13 dc, † skip next dc, work BPtr around next FPtr, ch 1, dc in next ch-1 sp and in next 4 dc, ch 3, skip next 2 dc and next ch-3 sp, work (2-tr Cluster, ch 3, 3 sc, ch 3, 2-tr Cluster) in next ch-3 sp, ch 3, skip next ch-3 sp and next 2 dc, dc in next 4 dc and in next ch-1 sp, ch 1, work BPtr around next FPtr, skip next dc †, dc in next 15 sts, work BPtr around same FPtr just worked into, ch 1, skip next dc, dc in next 2 dc and in next 2 chs, ch 2, skip next 2 Puff Sts, work (Puff St, ch 3, Puff St) in next ch-2 sp, ch 2, skip next ch-2 sp and first 2 chs of next ch-4, dc in next 2 chs and in next 2 dc, ch 1, skip next dc, work BPtr around next FPtr, dc in same FPtr just worked around and in next 14 dc, repeat from † to † once, dc in next 13 dc, work BPtr around last dc worked into.

Row 10: Ch 2, turn; dc in next 12 dc, † skip next dc, work FPtr around next BPtr, ch 1, dc in next ch-1 sp and in next 3 dc, ch 3, skip next 2 dc and next ch-3 sp, work (3-dc Cluster, ch 2, 3-dc Cluster) in next ch-3 sp, ch 4, work (3-dc Cluster, ch 2, 3-dc Cluster) in next ch-3 sp, ch 3, skip next ch-3 sp and next 2 dc, dc in next 3 dc and in next ch-1 sp, ch 1, work FPtr around next BPtr, skip next dc †, dc in next 15 sts and in next ch-1 sp, work FPtr around last BPtr worked into, ch 1, skip next 2 dc, dc in next 2 dc, ch 3, skip next ch-2 sp, sc in next ch-3 sp, ch 3, dc in next 2 dc, ch 1, skip next 2 dc and next ch-1 sp, work FPtr around next BPtr, working **behind** FPtr just made, dc in skipped ch-1 sp and in last BPtr worked around, dc in next 14 dc, repeat from † to † once, dc in last 12 dc, work FPtr around last dc worked into: 93 sts and 18 sps.

Row 11: Ch 2, turn; dc in next 11 dc, † skip next dc, work BPtr around next FPtr, ch 1, dc in next ch-1 sp and in next 3 dc, ch 3, skip next ch-3 sp, work (3-dc Cluster, ch 2, 3-dc Cluster) in next ch-2 sp, ch 4, sc in next ch-4 sp, ch 4, work (3-dc Cluster, ch 2, 3-dc Cluster) in next ch-2 sp, ch 3, skip next dc, dc in next 3 dc and in next ch-1 sp, ch 1, work BPtr around next FPtr, skip next dc †, dc in next 16 sts and in next ch-1 sp, working **behind** dc just made, work BPtr around last FPtr worked into, ch 1, skip next 2 dc, sc in next 2 chs, ch 3, skip next sc and next ch, sc in next 2 chs, ch 1, skip next 2 dc and next ch-1 sp, work BPtr around next FPtr, working in **front** of BPtr just made, dc in skipped ch-1 sp and in last FPtr worked around, dc in next 15 dc, repeat from † to † once, dc in next 11 dc, work BPtr around last dc worked into: 94 sts and 19 sps.

Row 12: Ch 2, turn; dc in next 10 dc, † skip next dc, work FPtr around next BPtr, ch 1, dc in next ch-1 sp and in next 3 dc, ch 3, skip next dc and next ch-3 sp, work (3-dc Cluster, ch 2, 3-dc Cluster) in next ch-2 sp, ch 4, skip next ch-4 sp, (dc, ch 2, dc) in next sc, ch 4, skip next ch-4 sp, work (3-dc Cluster, ch 2, 3-dc Cluster) in next ch-2 sp, ch 3, skip next ch-3 sp and next dc, dc in next 3 dc and in next ch-1 sp, ch 1, work FPtr around next BPtr, skip next dc †, dc in next 17 sts and in next ch-1 sp, working in **front** of last st made, work FPtr around last BPtr worked into, ch 1, skip next 2 sc, dc in next ch, sc in next ch, dc in next ch, ch 1, skip next 2 sc and next ch-1 sp, work FPtr around next BPtr, working **behind** FPtr just made, dc in skipped ch-1 sp and in last BPtr worked around, dc in next 16 dc, repeat from † to † once, dc in next 10 dc, work FPtr around last dc worked into: 95 sts and 20 sps.

Row 13: Ch 2, turn; dc in next 10 dc, † work BPtr around next FPtr, ch 1, dc in next 4 dc, ch 3, skip next ch-3 sp, work 3-dc Cluster in next ch-2 sp, ch 4, skip next ch-4 sp, work Puff St in next ch-2 sp (ch 2, Puff St) twice in same sp, ch 4, skip next ch-4 sp, work 3-dc Cluster in next ch-2 sp, ch 3, dc in next 4 dc, ch 1, work BPtr around next FPtr †, dc in next 19 sts and in next ch-1 sp, working **behind** dc just made, work BPtr around last FPtr worked into, ch 1, skip next 3 sts and next ch-1 sp, work BPtr around next FPtr, working in **front** of BPtr just made, dc in skipped ch-1 sp and in last FPtr worked around, dc in next 18 dc, repeat from † to † once, dc in next 10 dc, work BPtr around last dc worked into: 94 sts and 17 sps.

Row 14: Ch 2, turn; dc in next 10 dc, † work FPtr around next BPtr, ch 1, dc in next 4 dc and in next ch, ch 3, skip next 3-dc Cluster, sc in next ch-4 sp, ch 3, work (Puff St, ch 2) twice in next ch-2 sp, work (Puff St, ch 2, Puff St) in next ch-2 sp, ch 3, sc in next ch-4 sp, ch 3, skip next 3-dc Cluster and next 2 chs, dc in next ch and in next 4 dc, ch 1, work FPtr around next BPtr †, dc in next 20 dc, skip next BPtr, work FPdtr around next BPtr, ch 1, working in **front** of FPdtr just made, work FPdtr around skipped BPtr, dc in next 20 dc, repeat from † to † once, dc in next 10 dc, work FPtr around last dc worked into: 100 sts and 19 sps.

Row 15: Ch 2, turn; dc in next 10 dc, † work BPtr around next FPtr, ch 1, dc in next 5 dc and in next 2 chs, ch 3, skip next sc and next ch-3 sp, work (Puff St, ch 2) twice in next ch-2 sp, skip next ch-2 sp, work (Puff St, ch 2, Puff St) in next ch-2 sp, ch 4, skip next sc and next ch, dc in next 2 chs and in next 5 dc, ch 1, work BPtr around next FPtr †, dc in next 18 dc, skip next 2 dc, work BPtr around next FPdtr, ch 1, dc in same FPdtr just worked around, dc in next ch-1 sp and in next FPdtr, ch 1, work BPtr around same FPdtr just worked into, skip next 2 dc, dc in next 18 dc, repeat from † to † once, dc in next 10 dc, work BPtr around last dc worked into: 103 sts and 16 sps.

Row 16: Ch 2, turn; dc in next 10 dc, † dc in next BPtr, work FPtr around same BPtr just worked into, ch 1, skip next dc, dc in next 6 dc and in next ch, ch 3, work Puff St in next ch-2 sp, ch 2, (work Puff St, ch 2) twice in next ch-2 sp, work Puff St in next ch-2 sp, ch 3, skip next 2 chs, dc in next ch and in next 6 dc, ch 1, skip next dc, work FPtr around next BPtr, dc in same BPtr just worked around †, dc in next 16 dc, skip next 2 dc, work FPtr around next BPtr, ch 1, dc in same BPtr just worked around, dc in next ch-1 sp and in next 3 dc, dc in next ch-1 sp and in next BPtr, ch 1, work FPtr around same BPtr just worked into, skip next 2 dc, dc in next 16 dc, repeat from † to † once, dc in next 10 dc, work FPtr around last dc worked into: 107 sts and 16 sps.

Row 17: Ch 2, turn; dc in next 11 dc, † dc in next FPtr, work BPtr around FPtr just worked into, ch 1, skip next dc, dc in next 6 dc, ch 2, skip next ch-3 sp, work (Puff St, ch 1, Puff St) in next ch-2 sp, ch 2, skip next ch-2 sp, work (Puff St, ch 1, Puff St) in next ch-2 sp, ch 2, skip next ch-3 sp, dc in next 6 dc, ch 1, skip next dc, work BPtr around next FPtr, dc in same FPtr just worked around †, dc in next 15 dc, skip next 2 dc, work BPtr around next FPtr, ch 1, dc in same FPtr just worked around, dc in next ch-1 sp and in next 2 dc, ch 1, skip next dc, dc in next dc, ch 1, skip next dc, dc in next 2 dc and in next ch-1 sp, dc in next FPtr, ch 1, work BPtr around FPtr just worked into, skip next 2 dc, dc in next 15 dc, repeat from † to † once, dc in next 11 dc, work BPtr around last dc worked into: 105 sts and 18 sps.

Row 18: Ch 2, turn; dc in next 12 dc, † dc in next BPtr, work FPtr around BPtr just worked into, ch 1, skip next dc, dc in next 5 dc and in next ch, ch 4, skip next 2 Puff sts, work (Puff St, ch 3, Puff St) in next ch-2 sp, ch 4, skip next 2 Puff Sts and next ch, dc in next ch and in next 5 dc, ch 1, skip next dc, work FPtr around next BPtr, dc in same BPtr just worked around †, dc in next 14 dc, skip next 2 dc, work FPtr around next BPtr, ch 1, dc in same BPtr just worked around, dc in next ch-1 sp and in next 2 dc, ch 2, skip next 2 dc, (dc, ch 2) twice in next dc, skip next 2 dc, dc in next 2 dc, dc in next ch-1 sp and in next BPtr, ch 1, work FPtr around same BPtr just worked into, skip next 2 dc, dc in next 14 dc, repeat from † to † once, dc in next 12 dc, work FPtr around last dc worked into: 102 sts and 15 sps.

Row 19: Ch 2, turn; dc in next 13 dc, † dc in next FPtr, work BPtr around same FPtr just worked into, ch 1, skip next dc, dc in next 5 dc and in next ch, ch 3, sc in next ch-3 sp, ch 3, skip next 3 chs, dc in next ch and in next 5 dc, ch 1, skip next dc, work BPtr around next FPtr, dc in same FPtr just worked around †, dc in next 14 dc, skip next dc, work BPtr around next FPtr, ch 1, dc in next ch-1 sp and in next 3 dc, ch 2, skip next ch-2 sp, (work Puff St, ch 2) 3 times in next ch-2 sp, skip next ch-2 sp and next dc, dc in next 3 dc and in next ch-1 sp, ch 1, work BPtr around next FPtr, skip next dc, dc in next 14 dc, repeat from † to † once, dc in next 13 dc, work BPtr around last dc worked into: 103 sts and 14 sps.

Row 20: Ch 2, turn; dc in next 14 dc, † dc in next BPtr, work FPtr around BPtr just worked into, ch 1, skip next dc, dc in next 4 dc, hdc in next dc, sc in next 2 chs, ch 3, skip next sc and next ch, sc in next 2 chs, hdc in next dc, dc in next 4 dc, ch 1, skip next dc, work FPtr around next BPtr, dc in same BPtr just worked around †, dc in next 15 dc, work FPtr around next BPtr, ch 1, dc in next 3 dc, ch 4, skip next dc and next ch-2 sp, work (Puff St, ch 2) twice in next ch-2 sp, work (Puff St, ch 2, Puff St) in next ch-2 sp, ch 4, skip next ch-2 sp and next dc, dc in next 3 dc, ch 1, work FPtr around next BPtr, dc in next 15 dc, repeat from † to † once, dc in next 14 dc, work FPtr around last dc worked into: 108 sts and 13 sps.

Row 21: Ch 2, turn; dc in next 15 dc, † dc in next FPtr, work BPtr around FPtr just worked into, ch 1, skip next dc, dc in next 6 sts, hdc in next ch, sc in next ch, hdc in next ch, dc in next 6 sts, ch 1, skip next dc, work BPtr around next FPtr, dc in same FPtr just worked around †, dc in next 17 sts, work BPtr around same FPtr just worked into, ch 1, skip next dc, dc in next 2 dc and in next 2 chs, ch 2, skip next 2 Puff Sts, work (Puff St, ch 3, Puff St) in next ch-2 sp, ch 2, skip next ch-2 sp and first 2 chs of next ch-4, dc in next 2 chs and in next 2 dc, ch 1, skip next dc, work BPtr around next FPtr, dc in same FPtr just worked around and in next 16 dc, repeat from † to † once, dc in next 15 dc, work BPtr around last dc worked into: 116 sts and 9 sps.

Row 22: Ch 2, turn; dc in next 16 dc, † dc in next BPtr and in next ch-1 sp, working in **front** of last st made, work FPtr around same BPtr just worked into, ch 1, skip next 2 dc, dc in next 11 sts, ch 1, skip next 2 dc and next ch-1 sp, work FPtr around next BPtr, working **behind** FPtr just made, dc in skipped ch-1 sp and in last BPtr worked around †, dc in next 19 sts and in next ch-1 sp, working in **front** of last st made, work FPtr around last BPtr worked into, ch 1, skip next 2 dc, dc in next 2 dc, ch 3, skip next ch-2 sp, sc in next ch-3 sp, ch 3, dc in next 2 dc, ch 1, skip next 2 dc and next ch-1 sp, work FPtr around next BPtr, working **behind** FPtr just made, dc in skipped ch-1 sp and in last BPtr worked around, dc in next 18 dc, repeat from † to † once, dc in next 16 dc, work FPtr around last dc worked into: 115 sts and 8 sps.

Row 23: Ch 2, turn; dc in next 18 dc, † dc in next FPtr and in next ch-1 sp, working **behind** dc just made, work BPtr around last FPtr worked into, ch 1, skip next 2 dc, dc in next 7 dc, ch 1, skip next 2 dc and next ch-1 sp, work BPtr around next FPtr, working in **front** of BPtr just made, dc in skipped ch-1 sp and in last FPtr worked around †, dc in next 23 sts and in next ch-1 sp, working **behind** dc just made, work BPtr around last FPtr worked into, ch 1, skip next 2 dc, sc in next 2 chs, ch 3, skip next sc and next ch, sc in next 2 chs, ch 1, skip next 2 dc and next ch-1 sp, work BPtr around next FPtr, working in **front** of BPtr just made, dc in skipped ch-1 sp and in last FPtr just worked around, dc in next 22 dc, repeat from † to † once, dc in next 18 dc, work BPtr around last dc worked into: 118 sts and 7 sps.

Row 24: Ch 2, turn; dc in next 20 dc, † dc in next BPtr and in next ch-1 sp, working in **front** of last st made, work FPtr around last BPtr worked into, ch 1, skip next 2 dc, dc in next 3 dc, ch 1, skip next 2 dc and next ch-1 sp, work FPtr around next BPtr, working **behind** FPtr just made, dc in skipped ch-1 sp and in same BPtr just worked around †, dc in next 27 sts and in next ch-1 sp, working in **front** of last st made, work FPtr around last BPtr worked into, ch 1, skip next 2 sc, dc in next ch, sc in next ch, dc in next ch, ch 1, skip next 2 sc and next ch-1 sp, work FPtr around next BPtr, working **behind** FPtr just made, dc in skipped ch-1 sp and in last BPtr worked around, dc in next 26 dc, repeat from † to † once, dc in next 20 dc, work FPtr around last dc worked into: 121 sts and 6 ch-1 sps.

Row 25: Ch 2, turn; dc in next 22 dc, ★ † dc in next FPtr and in next ch-1 sp, working **behind** st just made, work BPtr around last FPtr worked into, ch 1, skip next 3 sts and next ch-1 sp, work BPtr around next FPtr, working in **front** of BPtr just made, dc in skipped ch-1 sp and in last FPtr worked around †, dc in next 30 dc; repeat from ★ once **more**, then repeat from † to † once; dc in next 22 dc, work BPtr around last dc worked into: 124 sts and 3 ch-1 sps.

Row 26: Ch 2, turn; dc in next 24 dc, ★ † skip next BPtr, work FPdtr around next BPtr, ch 1, working in **front** of FPdtr just made, work FPdtr around first skipped BPtr †, dc in next 34 dc; repeat from ★ once **more**, then repeat from † to † once, dc in next 24 dc, work FPtr around last dc worked into: 124 sts and 3 ch-1 sps.

Rows 27-98: Repeat Rows 3-26, 3 times.

Finish off.

FRINGE

Using photo as a guide for placement and holding 12 strands of yarn together, each 16" (40.5 cm) long, add fringe evenly spaced across short edges of Afghan ***(Figs. 6a & b, page 47)***.

GIRLIE FISHERMAN

Finished Size: 45" x 66"
(114.5 cm x 167.5 cm)

INTERMEDIATE

SHOPPING LIST

Yarn (Medium Weight) 4

[3.5 ounces, 170 yards (100 grams, 156 meters) per skein]:

- ☐ 17 skeins

Crochet Hook

- ☐ Size J (6 mm) **or** size needed for gauge

GAUGE INFORMATION

11 dc and 6 rows = 4" (10 cm)

Gauge Swatch: 4" (10 cm) square

Ch 13.

Row 1: Dc in fourth ch from hook **(3 skipped chs count as first dc)** and in each ch across: 11 dc.

Rows 2-6: Ch 2 **(counts as first dc)**, turn; dc in next dc and in each dc across.

Finish off.

STITCH GUIDE

DOUBLE TREBLE CROCHET ***(abbreviated dtr)***

YO 3 times, insert hook in st indicated YO and pull up a loop (5 loops on hook), (YO and draw through 2 loops on hook) 4 times.

FRONT POST TREBLE CROCHET ***(abbreviated FPtr)***

YO twice, insert hook from **front** to **back** around post of st indicated ***(Fig. 3, page 47)***, YO and pull up a loop (4 loops on hook), (YO and draw through 2 loops on hook) 3 times.

BACK POST TREBLE CROCHET ***(abbreviated BPtr)***

YO twice, insert hook from **back** to **front** around post of st indicated ***(Fig. 3, page 47)***, YO and pull up a loop (4 loops on hook), (YO and draw through 2 loops on hook) 3 times.

BACK POST TREBLE CROCHET 2 TOGETHER ***(abbreviated BPtr2tog)*** (uses next 2 FPtr)

★ YO twice, insert hook from **back** to **front** around post of next FPtr ***(Fig. 3, page 47)***, YO and pull up a loop (4 loops on hook), (YO and draw through 2 loops on hook) twice; repeat from ★ once **more**, YO and draw through all 3 loops on hook **(counts as one BPtr)**.

FRONT POST DOUBLE TREBLE CROCHET ***(abbreviated FPdtr)***

YO 3 times, insert hook from **front** to **back** around post of st indicated ***(Fig. 3, page 47)***, YO and pull up a loop (5 loops on hook), (YO and draw through 2 loops on hook) 4 times.

BACK POST DOUBLE TREBLE CROCHET ***(abbreviated BPdtr)***

YO 3 times, insert hook from **back** to **front** around post of st indicated ***(Fig. 3, page 47)***, YO and pull up a loop (5 loops on hook), (YO and draw through 2 loops on hook) 4 times.

BACK POST TRIPLE TREBLE CROCHET ***(abbreviated BPtrtr)***

YO 4 times, insert hook from **back** to **front** around post of st indicated ***(Fig. 3, page 47)***, YO and pull up a loop (6 loops on hook), (YO and draw through 2 loops on hook) 5 times.

5-DC POPCORN (uses one st)

5 Dc in st indicated, drop loop from hook, insert hook in first dc of 5-dc group, hook dropped loop and draw through st. On **wrong** side rows, insert hook from **back** to **front** in first dc of 5-dc group and complete in same manner.

6-DC POPCORN (uses one st)

6 Dc in st indicated, drop loop from hook, insert hook in first dc of 6-dc group, hook dropped loop and draw through st. On **wrong** side rows/rnds, insert hook from **back** to **front** in first dc of 6-dc group and complete in same manner.

FLOWER (uses one dc)

Work FPdtr around next dc, work 6-dc Popcorn in same dc, working **below** first FPdtr, work FPdtr around same dc **(counts as 3 sts)**.

PUFF STITCH ***(abbreviated Puff St)*** (uses one st or sp)

★ YO, insert hook in st or sp indicated, YO and pull up a loop even with loops on hook; repeat from ★ 4 times **more**, YO and draw through all 11 loops on hook.

6-DC CLUSTER (uses one st)

★ YO, insert hook in st indicated, YO and pull up a loop, YO and draw through 2 loops on hook; repeat from ★ 5 times **more**, YO and draw through all 7 loops on hook.

PANEL PATTERNS

SMALL CABLE (uses 4 sts)

Row 1: Skip next dc and next 2 chs, work FPdtr around next dc, working **behind** FPdtr just made, dc in first skipped ch; working in **front** of sts just made, work FPdtr around first skipped dc: 3 sts.

Row 2: Work BPtr around next FPdtr, work 6-dc Cluster in Back Loop Only of next dc *(Fig. 1, page 46)*, ch 1 **(counts as a st)**, work BPtr around next FPdtr: 4 sts.

Row 3: Skip next 3 sts, work FPdtr around next BPtr, working **behind** FPdtr just made, dc in skipped ch; working in **front** of sts just made, work FPdtr around first skipped BPtr.

Repeat Rows 2 and 3 for pattern.

BOUQUET PANEL (uses 16 sts)

Row 1: Dc in next 16 dc.

Row 2: Dc in next 6 dc, skip next 3 dc, work BPtrtr around next dc, ch 1 (does **not** count as a st), working in **front** of BPtrtr just made, dc in second skipped dc, working **behind** last 2 sts made, work BPtrtr around first skipped dc, dc in same dc as first BPtrtr worked around and in next 6 dc.

Row 3: Dc in next 5 dc, skip next 2 dc, work FPtr around each of next 2 sts, working **behind** 2 FPtr just made, dc in each st just worked around, working **below** second FPtr, work FPtr around same st, work FPtr around next BPtrtr, skip next dc, dc in next 5 dc.

Row 4: Dc in next 3 dc, skip next 2 dc, work BPdtr around each of next 2 FPtr, working in **front** of 2 BPtr just made, dc in each st just worked around and in next 4 sts, working **behind** sts just made, work BPdtr around each of 2 FPtr just worked into, skip next 2 dc, dc in next 3 dc.

Row 5: Dc in next 2 dc, skip next dc, work FPtr around each of next 2 sts, working **behind** last FPtr made, dc in last BPdtr worked around and in next 2 dc, ch 1 **(counts as a st)**, work 5-dc Popcorn in next dc, ch 1 **(counts as a st)**, skip next dc, dc in next 3 sts, working in **front** of last dc made, work FPtr around same BPdtr just worked into, work FPtr around next BPdtr, skip next dc, dc in next 2 dc: 17 sts.

Row 6: Dc in next 2 dc, BPtr2tog, working in **front** of last st made, dc in second FPtr worked around, dc in next dc, skip next dc, work 5-dc Popcorn in next dc, ch 1 **(counts as a st)**, skip next ch, work Puff St in next 5-dc Popcorn, ch 1 **(counts as a st)**, skip next ch, work 5-dc Popcorn in next dc, ch 1 **(counts as a st)**, dc in next 3 sts, working **behind** sts just made, BPtr2tog beginning first leg around same FPtr just worked into, dc in next 2 dc: 17 sts.

Row 7: Dc in next 3 sts, working in **front** of dc just made, work FPtr around first leg of same BPtr2tog just worked into, skip next dc, dc in next 3 sts, skip next 5-dc Popcorn, work 5-dc Popcorn in next ch, ch 1 **(counts as a st)**, dc in next 3 sts, skip next dc, work FPtr around second leg of next BPtr2tog, working **behind** FPtr just made, dc in same BPtr2tog just worked around and in next 2 dc: 16 sts.

Row 8: Dc in next 16 sts.

Repeat Rows 1-8 for pattern.

PANEL PATTERNS

TINY FLOWERS PANEL (uses 13 sts)
Row 1: Dc in next 2 dc, † skip next dc, work Flower, skip next dc †, dc in next 3 sts, repeat from † to † once, skip next dc, dc in next 2 dc.
Row 2: Dc in next 3 sts, hdc in next 6-dc Popcorn, dc in next 5 sts, hdc in next 6-dc Popcorn, dc in next 3 sts.
Row 3: Dc in next 5 sts, skip next dc, work Flower, skip next dc, dc in next 5 sts.
Row 4: Dc in next 6 sts, hdc in next 6-dc Popcorn, dc in next 6 sts.
Repeat Rows 1-4 for pattern.

LARGE CABLE PANEL (uses 11 sts)
Row 1: Dc in next 4 sts, working in **front** of dc just made, work FPtr around last st worked into, skip next dc, dc in next dc, skip next dc, work FPtr around next st, working **behind** FPtr just made, dc in same st just worked around and in next 3 dc.
Row 2: Dc in next 4 dc, skip next 2 sts, work BPdtr around next FPtr, working in **front** of BPdtr just made, dc in second skipped st, working **behind** sts just made, work BPdtr around first skipped FPtr, dc in next 4 dc.
Row 3: Dc in next 3 dc, skip next dc, work FPtr around next BPdtr, working **behind** FPtr just made, dc in same BPdtr just worked around and in next 2 sts, working in **front** of last dc made, work FPtr around same BPdtr just worked into, skip next dc, dc in next 3 dc.
Row 4: Dc in next 2 dc, skip next dc, work BPtr around next FPtr, working in **front** of BPtr just made, dc in same FPtr just worked around and in next 4 sts, working **behind** dc just made, work BPtr around same FPtr just worked into, skip next dc, dc in next 2 dc.
Row 5: Dc in next 2 dc, work FPtr around next BPtr, dc in next dc, skip next dc, work Flower, skip next dc, dc in next dc, work FPtr around next BPtr, dc in next 2 dc.
Row 6: Dc in next 3 sts, working **behind** last dc made, work BPtr around same FPtr just worked into, skip next dc, dc in next FPdtr, dc in next Popcorn and in next FPdtr, skip next dc, work BPtr around next FPtr, working in **front** of BPtr just made, dc in same FPtr just worked around and in next 2 dc.
Repeat Rows 1-6 for pattern.

AFGHAN

Tip: Work beginning ch with a larger size hook. Any extra looseness will be eased while working Bottom Edging.

Ch 126, place marker in first ch from hook for st placement.

Foundation Row: Slip st in third ch from hook, ch 3 **(counts as ch-3 sp)**, dc in next 2 chs, ch 2, skip next ch, dc in next 18 chs, ch 2, skip next ch, dc in next 15 chs, ch 2, skip next ch, dc in next 13 chs, ch 2, skip next ch, dc in next 18 chs, ch 2, skip next ch, dc in next 13 chs, ch 2, skip next ch, dc in next 15 chs, ch 2, skip next ch, dc in next 18 chs, ch 2, skip next ch, dc in next 2 chs, (hdc, dtr) in last ch: 133 sts and one ch-3 sp.

Row 1 (Right side)**:** Ch 3 **(counts as ch-3 sp, now and throughout)**, turn; skip first dtr, dc in next 2 sts, work Row 1 of following panels: **Small Cable, Bouquet, Small Cable, Tiny Flowers, Small Cable, Large Cable, Small Cable, Bouquet, Small Cable, Large Cable, Small Cable, Tiny Flowers, Small Cable, Bouquet, Small Cable**; dc in next dc, sc in last ch-3 sp, dtr in marked ch, do **not** remove marker.

Note: Loop a short piece of yarn around any stitch to mark Row 1 as **right** side.

Rows 2-95: Ch 3, turn; skip first dtr, dc in next 2 sts, work **next** row of following panels: **Small Cable, Bouquet, Small Cable, Tiny Flowers, Small Cable, Large Cable, Small Cable, Bouquet, Small Cable, Large Cable, Small Cable, Tiny Flowers, Small Cable, Bouquet, Small Cable**; dc in next dc, skip last dc, sc in last ch-3 sp, dtr in first ch of same ch-3 sp.

Row 96: Ch 3, turn; dc in next 2 sts, † work BPtr around next FPdtr, work 6-dc Cluster in Back Loop Only of next dc, work BPtr around next FPdtr †, dc in next 16 dc, repeat from † to † once, dc in next 6 sts, hdc in next st, dc in next 6 sts, repeat from † to † once, dc in next 11 sts, repeat from † to † once, dc in next 6 sts, hdc in next st, dc in next 6 sts, repeat from † to † once, dc in next 11 sts, repeat from † to † once, dc in next 16 sts, repeat from † to † once, dc in next 16 dc, repeat from † to † once, dc in next dc, skip last dc, sc in last ch-3 sp, dtr in first ch of same ch-3 sp, do **not** finish off: 126 sts.

TOP EDGING

Row 1: Turn; slip st in first dtr, ch 5, skip next 4 sts, slip st in next st, ch 3, skip next 2 sts, slip st in next st, ch 5, ★ skip next 2 sts, slip st in next st, ch 3, skip next 2 sts, slip st in next st, ch 5; repeat from ★ across to last 3 sts, skip next 3 sts, slip st in first ch of last ch-3 sp, ch 2, work FPtr around dtr one row **below**.

Row 2: Ch 3, turn; skip first FPtr and next ch-2 sp, dc in next slip st, ch 3, sc in next ch-5 sp, ★ (dc, ch 6, dc) in next ch-3 sp, sc in next ch-5 sp; repeat from ★ across to last slip st, ch 3, (dc, ch 3) twice in last slip st, slip st around dtr one row **below**; finish off.

BOTTOM EDGING

Row 1: With **right** side facing and working in free loops of beginning ch *(Fig. 2b, page 46)*; join yarn with slip st in marked ch, remove marker, ch 5, skip next 3 chs, slip st in next ch, ch 3, skip next 2 chs, slip st in next ch, ch 5, ★ skip next 2 chs, slip st in next ch, ch 3, skip next 2 chs, slip st in next ch, ch 5; repeat from ★ across to last 4 chs, skip next 3 chs, slip st in last ch, ch 2, work FPtr around dtr on Row 1.

Row 2: Ch 3, turn; skip first FPtr and next ch-2 sp, dc in next slip st, ch 3, sc in next ch-5 sp, ★ (dc, ch 6, dc) in next ch-3 sp, sc in next ch-5 sp; repeat from ★ across to joining slip st, ch 3, (dc, ch 3) twice in joining slip st, slip st around dtr on Row 2; finish off.

MOSTLY POSTS

Finished Size: 40" x 62"
(101.5 cm x 157.5 cm)

INTERMEDIATE

SHOPPING LIST

Yarn (Medium Weight) 4
[5 ounces, 250 yards
(141.7 grams, 228 meters) per skein]:
☐ 12 skeins

Crochet Hook
☐ Size I (5.5 mm)
or size needed for gauge

GAUGE INFORMATION

13 dc and 7 rows = 4" (10 cm)
Gauge Swatch: 4" (10 cm) square
Ch 15.
Row 1: Dc in fourth ch from hook **(3 skipped chs count as first dc)** and in each ch across: 13 dc.
Rows 2-7: Ch 2 **(counts as first dc)**, turn; dc in next dc and in each dc across. Finish off.

STITCH GUIDE

TREBLE CROCHET ***(abbreviated tr)***
YO twice, insert hook in st indicated, YO and pull up a loop (4 loops on hook), (YO and draw through 2 loops on hook) 3 times.

FRONT POST TREBLE CROCHET ***(abbreviated FPtr)***
YO twice, insert hook from **front** to **back** around post of st indicated ***(Fig. 3, page 47)***, YO and pull up a loop (4 loops on hook), (YO and draw through 2 loops on hook) 3 times.

FRONT POST DOUBLE TREBLE CROCHET ***(abbreviated FPdtr)***
YO 3 times, insert hook from **front** to **back** around post of st indicated ***(Fig. 3, page 47)***, YO and pull up a loop (5 loops on hook), (YO and draw through 2 loops on hook) 4 times.

BACK POST DOUBLE TREBLE CROCHET ***(abbreviated BPdtr)***
YO 3 times, insert hook from **back** to **front** around post of st indicated ***(Fig. 3, page 47)***, YO and pull up a loop (5 loops on hook), (YO and draw through 2 loops on hook) 4 times.

FRONT POST TRIPLE TREBLE CROCHET ***(abbreviated FPtrtr)***
YO 4 times, insert hook from **front** to **back** around post of st indicated ***(Fig. 3, page 47)***, YO and pull up a loop (6 loops on hook), (YO and draw through 2 loops on hook) 5 times.

BACK POST TRIPLE TREBLE CROCHET ***(abbreviated BPtrtr)***
YO 4 times, insert hook from **back** to **front** around post of st indicated ***(Fig. 3, page 47)***, YO and pull up a loop (6 loops on hook), (YO and draw through 2 loops on hook) 5 times.

FRONT POST QUADRUPLE CROCHET ***(abbreviated FPqtr)***
YO 5 times, insert hook from **front** to **back** around post of st indicated ***(Fig. 3, page 47)***, YO and pull up a loop (7 loops on hook), (YO and draw through 2 loops on hook) 6 times.

FP CLUSTER
First Leg: YO 6 times, insert hook from **front** to **back** around post of dc 2 rows **below** next dc ***(Fig. 3, page 47)***, YO and pull a loop (8 loops on hook), (YO and draw through 2 loops on hook) 6 times (2 loops remaining on hook).
Second Leg: YO, working **behind** First Leg, insert hook in next dc, YO and pull up a loop (4 loops on hook), YO and draw through 2 loops on hook, YO and draw through all 3 loops on hook.

RIGHT SIDE EDGE STITCH ***(abbreviated RS edge st)***
YO, insert hook in last dc, YO and pull up a loop, YO and draw through 2 loops on hook (2 loops remaining on hook), YO twice, insert hook from **front** to **back** around post of next-to-last st on row **below** ***(Fig. 3, page 47)***, YO and pull up a loop (5 loops on hook), (YO and draw through 2 loops on hook) twice, YO and draw through all 3 loops on hook.

WRONG SIDE EDGE STITCH ***(abbreviated WS edge st)***
YO, insert hook in last dc, YO and pull up a loop, YO and draw through 2 loops on hook (2 loops remaining on hook), YO twice, insert hook from **back** to **front** around post of next-to-last st on row **below** ***(Fig. 3, page 47)***, YO and pull up a loop (5 loops on hook), (YO and draw through 2 loops on hook) twice, YO and draw through all 3 loops on hook.

PANEL STITCHES

RAISED V (uses 5 sts)

Row 1: Dc in next 2 dc, work FPtr around next dc, place marker in FPtr just made, dc in next 2 dc.

Row 2: Dc in next 3 sts, place marker in last dc made, dc in next 2 sts.

Row 3: Skip next 2 sts, work FPtrtr around marked st **below** next dc, remove marker, working **behind** FPtrtr just made, dc in second skipped dc and in next marked dc, do **not** remove marker, place marker in last dc made, dc in next dc, working **below** last FPtrtr made, work FPtrtr around same st, skip next st from last dc made.

Row 4: Skip next 2 sts, work BPtrtr around marked dc **below** next dc, remove marker, working in **front** of BPtrtr just made, dc in second skipped dc and in next marked dc, do **not** remove marker, place marker in last dc made, dc in next dc, working **below** last BPtrtr made, work BPtrtr around same st, skip next st from last dc made.

Repeat Rows 3 and 4 for pattern.

BRAID (uses 6 sts)

Row 1: Work FPdtr around each of next 2 sts, skip next 2 sts, work FPdtr around each of next 2 sts, working in **front** of last 2 FPdtr made, work FPdtr around each of 2 skipped sts.

Row 2: Work BPdtr around each of next 2 sts, skip next 2 sts, work BPdtr around each of next 2 sts, working **behind** last 2 BPdtr made, work BPdtr around each of 2 skipped sts.

Repeat Rows 1 and 2 for pattern.

ROPE (uses 7 sts)

Rows 1 and 2: Dc in next 7 dc.

Row 3: Dc in next dc, work 6 FP Clusters.

Row 4: Dc in next 7 sts.

Row 5: Dc in next dc, work 6 FP Clusters.

Repeat Rows 4 and 5 for pattern.

TWIST (uses 5 sts)

Row 1: Work FPtr around each of next 2 dc, dc in next dc, work FPtr around each of next 2 dc.

Row 2: Dc in next 5 sts.

Row 3: Skip next 3 dc, work FPqtr around each st one row **below** next 2 dc, working **behind** 2 FPqtr just made, dc in third skipped dc, working in **front** of 3 sts just made, work FPqtr around each st one row **below** first 2 skipped dc, skip next 2 dc from last dc made.

Repeat Rows 2 and 3 for pattern.

CABLE (uses 13 sts)

Row 1: Dc in next 4 dc, skip next 3 sts, work FPtrtr around each of next 2 sts, working **behind** 2 FPtrtr just made, dc in third skipped st, working in **front** of 3 sts just made, work FPtrtr around each of first 2 skipped sts, dc in next 4 dc.

Row 2: Dc in next 3 dc, skip next dc, work BPdtr around each of next 2 FPtrtr, dc in last FPtrtr worked around and in next 2 sts, work BPdtr around st just worked into, work BPdtr around next st, skip next dc, dc in next 3 dc.

Row 3: Dc in next 3 dc, work FPtr around each of next 2 BPdtr, dc in next 3 dc, work FPtr around each of next 2 BPdtr, dc in next 3 dc.

Row 4: Dc in next 4 sts, work BPdtr around last FPtr worked into, work BPdtr around next FPtr, skip next dc, dc in next dc, skip next dc, work BPdtr around each of next 2 FPtr, dc in last FPtr worked around and in next 3 dc.

Row 5: Repeat Row 1.

Row 6: Dc in next 4 dc, skip next 3 sts, work BPtrtr around each of next 2 FPtrtr, ch 1 **(counts as a st)**, working in **front** of 2 BPtrtr just made, work BPtrtr around each of first 2 skipped FPtrtr, leave third skipped st (dc) unworked, dc in next 4 dc.

Row 7: Dc in next 4 dc, skip next 3 sts, work FPtrtr around each of next 2 BPtrtr, working **behind** 2 FPtrtr just made, dc in skipped ch, working in **front** of 3 sts just made, work FPtrtr around each of first 2 skipped BPtrtr, dc in next 4 dc.

Repeat Rows 2-7 for pattern.

PANEL STITCHES

WIDE TWIST (uses 6 sts)
Row 1: Skip next 3 sts, work FPdtr around each of next 3 sts, working in **front** of 3 FPdtr just made, work FPdtr around each of 3 skipped sts.
Row 2: Work BPdtr around each of next 6 FPdtr.
Repeat Rows 1 and 2 for pattern.

LATTICE (uses 21 sts)
Row 1: Dc in next 3 dc, ★ † skip next 2 sts, work FPdtr around next st, working **behind** FPdtr just made, dc in second skipped st, working in **front** of 2 sts just made, work FPdtr around first skipped st †, skip next dc from last dc made, dc in next dc; repeat from ★ 2 times **more**, then repeat from † to † once, dc in next 3 dc.
Row 2: Dc in next 3 dc, work BPdtr around next FPdtr, dc in next dc, ★ skip next 2 sts, work BPdtr around next FPdtr, working in **front** of BPdtr just made, dc in second skipped st, working **behind** 2 sts just made, work BPdtr around first skipped st, dc in next dc; repeat from ★ 2 times **more**, work BPdtr around next FPdtr, dc in next 3 dc.
Repeat Rows 1 and 2 for pattern.

AFGHAN

Tip: Work beginning ch with a larger size hook. Any extra looseness will be eased while working Bottom Edging.

Ch 132, place marker in third ch from hook for st placement.

Foundation Row (Wrong side)**:** Dc in fourth ch from hook **(3 skipped chs count as first dc)** and in each ch across: 130 dc.

Note: Loop a short piece of yarn around **back** of any stitch on Foundation Row to mark **right** side.

Row 1: Ch 2 **(counts as first dc, now and throughout)**, turn; dc in next 2 dc, work Row 1 of **Raised V**, dc in next 3 dc, work Row 1 of **Braid**, dc in next 3 dc, work Row 1 of **Rope**, dc in next 3 dc, work Row 1 of (**Twist**, **Cable**, **Wide Twist**, **Lattice**, **Wide Twist**, **Cable**, **Twist**), dc in next 3 dc, work Row 1 of **Rope**, dc in next 3 dc, work Row 1 of **Braid,** dc in next 3 dc, work Row 1 of **Raised V**, dc in next 3 dc, work RS edge st.

Row 2: Ch 2, turn; dc in next 3 dc, work next row of **Raised V**, dc in next 3 dc, work next row of **Braid**, dc in next 3 dc, work next row of **Rope**, dc in next 3 dc, work next row of (**Twist**, **Cable**, **Wide Twist**, **Lattice**, **Wide Twist**, **Cable**, **Twist**), dc in next 3 dc, work next row of **Rope**, dc in next 3 dc, work next row of **Braid,** dc in next 3 dc, work next row of **Raised V**, dc in next 2 dc, work WS edge st.

Row 3: Ch 2, turn; dc in next 3 dc, work next row of **Raised V**, dc in next 3 dc, work next row of **Braid**, dc in next 3 dc, work next row of **Rope**, dc in next 3 dc, work next row of (**Twist**, **Cable**, **Wide Twist**, **Lattice**, **Wide Twist**, **Cable**, **Twist**), dc in next 3 dc, work next row of **Rope**, dc in next 3 dc, work next row of **Braid,** dc in next 3 dc, work next row of **Raised V**, dc in next 3 dc, work RS edge st.

Repeat Rows 2 and 3 for pattern until Body measures approximately 60½" (153.5 cm) from beginning ch ending by working Row 4 of Cable pattern.

Last Row: Ch 2, turn; dc in next 3 dc, work next row of **Raised V**, † dc in next 3 dc, work FPtr around each of next 2 sts, skip next 2 sts, work FPtr around each of next 2 sts, working in **front** of last 2 FPtr made, work FPtr around each of 2 skipped sts, dc in next 3 dc †, work next row of **Rope**, dc in next 3 dc, work next row of (**Twist**, **Cable**, **Wide Twist**, **Lattice**, **Wide Twist**, **Cable**, **Twist**), dc in next 3 dc, work next row of **Rope**, repeat from † to † once, work next row of **Raised V**, dc in next 3 dc, work RS edge st, do **not** finish off.

TOP EDGING

Row 1: Ch 1, turn; sc in each st across to last dc, insert hook in last dc, YO and pull up a loop, YO twice, insert hook from **back** to **front** around post of next-to-last st on row **below**, YO and pull up a loop (5 loops on hook), (YO and draw through 2 loops on hook) twice, YO and draw through all 3 loops on hook: 130 sts.

Row 2: Ch 3, turn; skip next 2 sc, tr in next sc, ch 3, working in **front** of last tr made, dtr in st **below** beginning ch-3, ★ skip next 2 sc, tr in next sc, ch 3, working in **front** of tr just made, tr in first skipped sc; repeat from ★ across to last 3 sc, skip next 2 sc, tr in last sc, ch 2, working in **front** of tr just made, tr in first skipped st, working **behind** first tr made, hdc in same st as first tr made; finish off.

BOTTOM EDGING

Row 1: With **wrong** side facing and working in free loops of beginning ch ***(Fig. 2b, page 46)***, join yarn with sc in marked ch ***(see Joining With Sc, page 46)***; remove marker, sc in each ch across: 130 sc.

Row 2: Turn; slip st in first sc, ch 2, skip next sc, tr in next sc, ch 1, working in **front** of tr just made, work FPdtr around first st on Row 1 of Body, ★ skip next 2 sc, tr in next sc, ch 3, working in **front** of tr just made, tr in first skipped sc; repeat from ★ across to last 4 sc, skip next 3 sc, tr in last sc, ch 2, working in **front** of tr just made, tr in first skipped sc, working **behind** first tr made, hdc in same st as first tr made; finish off.

A SHOWER OF LEAVES

Finished Size: 46½" x 65"
(118 cm x 165 cm)

INTERMEDIATE

SHOPPING LIST

Yarn (Medium Weight) 4

[5 ounces, 251 yards (142 grams, 230 meters) per skein]:
- ☐ 10 skeins

Crochet Hook
- ☐ Size J (6 mm) **or** size needed for gauge

Additional Supplies
- ☐ Lock-style stitch markers

GAUGE INFORMATION

11 dc and 6 rows = 4" (10 cm)
Gauge Swatch: 4" (10 cm) square
Ch 13.
Row 1: Dc in fourth ch from hook **(3 skipped chs count as first dc)** and in each ch across: 11 dc.
Rows 2-6: Ch 2 **(counts as first dc)**, turn; dc in next dc and in each dc across.
Finish off.

STITCH GUIDE

Note: To work a stitch with several yarn overs, YO **tightly** as many times as instructed. When working the loops off, be careful not to allow too much slack in the loops on the hook. Practice this a few times until you have an uniform stitch without a large loop at the end.

TRIPLE LEAF (uses 3 dc)
Working in **front** of previous row, ★ YO 3 times, insert hook in skipped dc 2 rows **below**, YO and pull up a loop, place marker through last 2 loops on hook, (YO and draw through 2 loops on hook) 3 times, YO twice, working in side two legs ***(Fig. 4, page 47)***, insert hook from **right** to **left** through both marked loops, YO and pull up a loop, (YO and draw through 2 loops) twice, remove marker; repeat from ★ 2 times **more**, YO and draw through all 7 loops on hook, ch 1 to close (closing ch does **not** count as a st).

DOUBLE LEAF (uses 2 dc)
Working in **front** of previous row, ★ YO 3 times, insert hook in skipped dc 2 rows **below**, YO and pull up a loop, place marker through last 2 loops on hook, (YO and draw through 2 loops on hook) 3 times, YO twice, working in side two legs ***(Fig. 4, page 47)***, insert hook from **right** to **left** through both marked loops, YO and pull up a loop, (YO and draw through 2 loops) twice, remove marker; repeat from ★ once **more**, YO and draw through all 5 loops on hook (Double Leaf does **not** count as a st).

LARGE LEAF
Working in **front** of previous rows, YO 6 times, insert hook in skipped dc 4 rows **below**, YO and pull up a loop, place marker through last 2 loops on hook, (YO and draw through 2 loops on hook) 6 times, YO and draw through one loop on hook (2 loops on hook), YO, insert hook in next dc on previous row, YO and pull up a loop, YO and draw through 2 loops on hook (3 loops on hook), YO 5 times, working in side two legs ***(Fig. 4, page 47)***, insert hook from **right** to **left** through both marked loops, remove marker, YO and pull up a loop, place marker through last 2 loops on hook, (YO and draw through 2 loops on hook) 5 times (4 loops on hook), YO 3 times, insert hook from **right** to **left** through both marked loops, remove marker, YO and pull up a loop, (YO and draw through 2 loops on hook) 3 times (5 loops on hook), YO, insert hook in **same** dc on previous row, YO and pull up a loop, (YO and draw through 2 loops on hook) twice, YO and draw through all 5 loops on hook.

TRIPLE LEAF PANEL

Ch 28.

Row 1 (Right side)**:** Dc in fourth ch from hook **(3 skipped chs count as first dc, now and throughout)** and in each ch across: 26 dc.

Note: Loop a short piece of yarn around any stitch to mark Row 1 as **right** side and bottom edge.

Row 2: Ch 3 **(counts as first dc, now and throughout)**, turn; dc in next 2 dc, † skip next dc, 2 dc in next dc, (dc in next dc, skip next dc, 2 dc in next dc) twice †, dc in next 6 dc, repeat from † to † once, dc in last dc.

Row 3: Ch 3, turn; dc in next 4 dc, work Triple Leaf, skip dc **behind** Triple Leaf, dc in next 13 dc, work Triple Leaf, skip dc **behind** Triple Leaf, dc in last 6 dc.

Row 4: Ch 3, turn; dc in next 9 sts, skip next dc, 2 dc in next dc, (dc in next dc, skip next dc, 2 dc in next dc) twice, dc in last 8 sts.

Row 5: Ch 3, dc in next 11 dc, work Triple Leaf, skip dc **behind** Triple Leaf, dc in last 13 dc.

Row 6: Ch 3, turn; dc in next 2 dc, † skip next dc, 2 dc in next dc, (dc in next dc, skip next dc, 2 dc in next dc) twice †, dc in next 6 sts, repeat from † to † once, dc in last dc.

Rows 7-97: Repeat Rows 3-6, 22 times; then repeat Rows 3-5 once **more**.

Row 98: Ch 3, turn; dc in next st and in each st across; finish off.

DOUBLE LEAF PANEL

(Make 4)

Ch 17.

Row 1 (Right side)**:** Dc in fourth ch from hook and in each ch across: 15 dc.

Note: Mark Row 1 as **right** side and bottom edge.

Row 2: Ch 3, turn; dc in next 8 dc, ★ skip next dc, 2 dc in next dc, dc in next dc; repeat from ★ once **more**.

Row 3: Ch 3, turn; dc in next 3 dc, work Double Leaf **(does not count as a st, now and throughout)**, dc in last 11 dc.

Row 4: Ch 3, turn; dc in next 5 dc, skip next dc, 2 dc in next dc, dc in next dc, skip next dc, 2 dc in next dc, dc in last 4 dc.

Row 5: Ch 3, turn; dc in next 6 dc, work Double Leaf, dc in last 8 dc.

Row 6: Ch 3, turn; dc in next 2 dc, skip next dc, 2 dc in next dc, dc in next dc, skip next dc, 2 dc in next dc, dc in last 7 dc.

Row 7: Ch 3, turn; dc in next 9 dc, work Double Leaf, dc in last 5 dc.

Rows 8 and 9: Repeat Rows 6 and 7.

Row 10: Ch 3, turn; dc in next 5 dc, skip next dc, 2 dc in next dc, dc in next dc, skip next dc, 2 dc in next dc, dc in last 4 dc.

Row 11: Ch 3, turn; dc in next 6 dc, work Double Leaf, dc in last 8 dc.

Row 12: Ch 3, turn; dc in next 8 dc, ★ skip next dc, 2 dc in next dc, dc in next dc; repeat from ★ once **more**.

Row 13: Ch 3, turn; dc in next 3 dc, work Double Leaf, dc in last 11 dc.

Rows 14-97: Repeat Rows 2-13, 7 times.

Row 98: Ch 3, turn; dc in next dc and in each dc across; finish off.

LARGE LEAF PANEL (Make 2)

Ch 23.

Row 1 (Right side)**:** Dc in fourth ch from hook and in each ch across: 21 dc.

Note: Mark Row 1 as **right** side and bottom edge.

Row 2: Ch 3, turn; dc in next 7 sts, skip next dc, 2 dc in next dc, dc in last 11 sts.

Row 3: Ch 3, turn; dc in next dc and in each dc across.

Row 4: Ch 3, turn; dc in next 3 dc, skip next dc, 2 dc in next dc, dc in next 10 sts, skip next dc, 2 dc in next dc, dc in last 3 sts.

Row 5: Ch 3, turn; dc in next 11 dc, work Large Leaf, dc in last 8 sts.

Row 6: Ch 3, turn; dc in next 11 sts, skip next dc, 2 dc in next dc, dc in last 7 sts.

Row 7: Ch 3, turn; dc in next 3 dc, work Large Leaf, dc in next 11 dc, work Large Leaf, dc in last 4 sts.

Row 8: Ch 3, turn; dc in next 7 sts, skip next dc, 2 dc in next dc, dc in last 11 sts.

Row 9: Ch 3, turn; dc in next 7 dc, work Large Leaf, dc in last 12 sts.

Rows 10-95: Repeat Rows 4-9, 14 times; then repeat Rows 4 and 5 once **more**.

Row 96: Ch 3, turn; dc in next dc and in each st across.

Row 97: Ch 3, turn; dc in next 3 dc, work Large Leaf, dc in next 11 dc, work Large Leaf, dc in last 4 sts.

Row 98: Ch 3, turn; dc in next dc and in each st across; finish off.

ASSEMBLY

Using Diagram as guide for placement, join two Panels as follows: With **wrong** sides and bottom edges together and working through ends of rows on **both** pieces, join yarn with slip st at bottom corner; ch 1, working from **left** to **right**, work reverse sc in first row *(Figs. 5a-d, page 47)*, work 2 reverse sc in next row, ★ work reverse sc in next row, work 2 reverse sc in next row; repeat from ★ across to last 2 rows, work reverse sc in last 2 rows, slip st in top of last st on Row 98; finish off.

Repeat with remaining Panels.

FIRST SIDE EDGING

With **right** side facing and working in ends of rows, join yarn with slip st in bottom corner; ch 1, working from **left** to **right**, work reverse sc in first row, work 2 reverse sc in next row, ★ work reverse sc in next row, work 2 reverse sc in next row; repeat from ★ across to last 2 rows, work reverse sc in last 2 rows, slip st in top of last st on Row 98; finish off.

SECOND SIDE EDGING

With **right** side facing and working in ends of rows, join yarn with slip st in last st on Row 98; ch 1, working from **left** to **right**, work reverse sc in first row, work 2 reverse sc in next row, ★ work reverse sc in next row, work 2 reverse sc in next row; repeat from ★ across to last 2 rows, work reverse sc in last 2 rows, slip st in last st at bottom corner; finish off.

FRINGE

Using photo as a guide for placement and holding 10 strands of yarn together, each 14" (35.5 cm) long, add 19 groups of fringe evenly spaced across each short edge of Afghan *(Figs. 6a & b, page 47)*.

DIAGRAM

Double Leaf	Large Leaf	Double Leaf	Triple Leaf	Double Leaf	Large Leaf	Double Leaf

WINDING PATHS

Finished Size: 42" x 59"
(106.5 cm x 150 cm)

INTERMEDIATE

SHOPPING LIST

Yarn (Medium Weight) MEDIUM 4
[3.5 ounces, 205 yards
(100 grams, 187 meters) per skein]:
☐ 10 skeins

Crochet Hook
☐ Size I (5.5 mm)
or size needed for gauge

GAUGE INFORMATION

13 dc and 7 rows = 4" (10 cm)
Gauge Swatch: 4" (10 cm) square
Ch 15.
Row 1: Dc in fourth ch from hook **(3 skipped chs count as first dc)** and in each ch across: 13 dc.
Rows 2-7: Ch 2 **(counts as first dc)**, turn; dc in next dc and in each dc across.
Finish off.

STITCH GUIDE

DOUBLE TREBLE CROCHET ***(abbreviated dtr)***
YO 3 times, insert hook in st indicated, YO and pull up a loop (5 loops on hook), (YO and draw through 2 loops on hook) 4 times.

FRONT POST TREBLE CROCHET ***(abbreviated FPtr)***
YO twice, insert hook from **front** to **back** around post of st indicated *(Fig. 3, page 47)*, YO and pull up a loop (4 loops on hook), (YO and draw through 2 loops on hook) 3 times.

BACK POST TREBLE CROCHET ***(abbreviated BPtr)***
YO twice, insert hook from **back** to **front** around post of st indicated *(Fig. 3, page 47)*, YO and pull up a loop (4 loops on hook), (YO and draw through 2 loops on hook) 3 times.

PUFF STITCH ***(abbreviated Puff St)*** (uses one st or sp)
★ YO, insert hook in st or sp indicated, YO and pull up a loop even with loop on hook; repeat from ★ 2 times **more**, YO and draw through all 7 loops on hook.

AFGHAN

Ch 139.

Row 1 (Right side)**:** Dc in fourth ch from hook **(3 skipped chs count as first dc)** and in each ch across: 137 dc.

Note: Loop a short piece of yarn around any stitch to mark Row 1 as **right** side.

Row 2: Ch 3 **(counts as first dc, now and throughout)**, turn; dc in next 14 dc, ★ † work BPtr around next dc, dc in next 6 dc, ch 2, skip next 2 dc, dc in next dc, ch 2, skip next 2 dc, dc in next 6 dc, work BPtr around next dc †, dc in next 10 dc, work BPtr around next dc, dc in next dc, ch 2, skip next 2 dc, dc in next dc, ch 3, skip next 2 dc, dc in next dc, work BPtr around next dc, dc in next 10 dc; repeat from ★ once **more**, then repeat from † to † once, dc in next 5 dc, hdc in next dc, work BPtr around same dc just worked into, leave last dc unworked **(now and throughout)**: 117 sts and 10 sps.

Row 3: Ch 3, turn; dc in next 6 sts, ★ † work FPtr around next BPtr, dc in next 3 dc, ch 2, skip next dc, sc in next dc, ch 3, skip next dc, (dc, ch 2, dc) in next dc, ch 3, skip next dc, sc in next dc, ch 2, skip next dc, dc in next 3 dc, work FPtr around next BPtr †, dc in next 10 dc, work FPtr around next BPtr, dc in next dc, ch 3, work (Puff St, ch 3) twice in next dc, dc in next dc, work FPtr around next BPtr, dc in next 10 dc; repeat from ★ once **more**, then repeat from † to † once, dc in next 13 dc, hdc in next dc, work FPtr around same dc just worked into: 110 sts and 21 sps.

Row 4: Ch 3, turn; dc in next 14 sts, ★ † work BPtr around next FPtr, dc in next 3 dc, ch 3, skip next 2 sps, work Puff St in next ch-2 sp, (ch 2, work Puff St in same sp) twice, ch 4, skip next sc, dc in next 3 dc, work BPtr around next FPtr †, dc in next 10 dc, work BPtr around next FPtr, dc in next dc, ch 2, skip next ch-3 sp, dc in next ch-3 sp, ch 3, dc in next dc, work BPtr around next FPtr, dc in next 10 dc; repeat from ★ once **more**, then repeat from † to † once, dc in next 5 dc, hdc in next dc, work BPtr around same dc just worked into: 105 sts and 16 sps.

Row 5: Ch 3, turn; dc in next 6 sts, ★ † work FPtr around next BPtr, dc in next 3 dc, ch 3, skip next ch-4 sp, work (Puff St, ch 2) twice in next ch-2 sp, work (Puff St, ch 2, Puff St) in next ch-2 sp, ch 3, dc in next 3 dc, work FPtr around next BPtr †, dc in next 10 dc, work FPtr around next BPtr, dc in next dc, ch 3, work (Puff St, ch 3) twice in next dc, dc in next dc, work FPtr around next BPtr, dc in next 10 dc; repeat from ★ once **more**, then repeat from † to † once, dc in next 13 dc, hdc in next dc, work FPtr around same dc just worked into: 110 sts and 21 sps.

Row 6: Ch 3, turn; dc in next 13 sts, ★ † skip next dc, work BPtr around next FPtr, dc in same FPtr just worked around and in next dc, ch 4, sc in next ch-3 sp, ch 4, skip next ch-2 sp, dc in next ch-2 sp, ch 4, skip next 2 Puff Sts and next 2 chs, dc in next ch and in next 2 dc, skip next dc, work BPtr around next FPtr †, dc in same FPtr just worked around and in next 9 dc, skip next dc, work BPtr around next FPtr, ch 2, dc in next ch-3 sp, ch 4, skip next 2 Puff Sts and next 2 chs, dc in next ch, skip next dc, work BPtr around next FPtr, dc in same FPtr just worked around and in next 9 dc; repeat from ★ once **more**, then repeat from † to † once, dc in same FPtr just worked around and in next 5 dc, hdc in next dc, work BPtr around same dc just worked into: 97 sts and 13 sps.

Row 7: Ch 3, turn; dc in next 8 sts, ★ † work FPtr around same BPtr just worked into, skip next dc, dc in next 2 dc and next 2 chs, ch 3, sc in next dc, ch 3, (dc, ch 2, dc) in next sc, ch 3, sc in next dc, ch 2, skip next dc, dc in next BPtr, work FPtr around same BPtr just worked into †, skip next dc, dc in next 10 sts, work FPtr around same BPtr just worked into, skip next dc, dc in next ch, ch 3, work (Puff St, ch 3) twice in next dc, dc in next BPtr, work FPtr around same BPtr just worked into, skip next dc, dc in next 10 sts; repeat from ★ once **more**, then repeat from † to † once, skip next dc, dc in next 11 dc, hdc in next dc, work FPtr around same dc just worked into: 107 sts and 21 sps.

Row 8: Ch 3, turn; dc in next 11 sts, ★ † skip next dc, work BPtr around next FPtr, dc in same FPtr just worked around and in next dc, ch 3, skip next 2 sps, work Puff St in next ch-2 sp, (ch 2, work Puff St in same sp) twice, ch 4, skip next sc and next 2 chs, dc in next ch and next 3 dc, skip next dc, work BPtr around next FPtr †, dc in same FPtr just worked around and in next 9 dc, skip next dc, work BPtr around next FPtr, ch 2, dc in next ch-3 sp, ch 4, skip next 2 Puff Sts and next 2 chs, dc in next ch, skip next dc, work BPtr around next FPtr, dc in same FPtr just worked around and in next 9 dc; repeat from ★ once **more**, then repeat from † to † once, dc in same FPtr just worked around and in next 7 dc, hdc in next dc, work BPtr around same dc just worked into: 103 sts and 16 sps.

Row 9: Ch 3, turn; dc in next 10 sts, ★ † work FPtr around same BPtr just worked into, skip next dc, dc in next 3 dc, ch 3, skip next ch-4 sp, work (Puff St, ch 2) twice in next ch-2 sp, work (Puff St, ch 2, Puff St) in next ch-2 sp, ch 3, skip next ch-3 sp, dc in next 3 sts, work FPtr around same BPtr just worked into †, skip next dc, dc in next 10 sts, work FPtr around last st worked into, skip next dc, dc in next ch, ch 3, work (Puff St, ch 3) twice in next dc, dc in next BPtr, work FPtr around same BPtr just worked into, skip next dc, dc in next 10 sts; repeat from ★ once **more**, then repeat from † to † once, skip next dc, dc in next 9 sts, hdc in next dc, work FPtr around same dc just worked into: 110 sts and 21 sps.

Row 10: Ch 3, turn; dc in next 9 sts, ★ † skip next dc, work BPtr around next FPtr, dc in same FPtr just worked around and in next dc, ch 4, sc in next ch-3 sp, ch 4, skip next ch-2 sp, dc in next ch-2 sp, ch 4, skip next 2 Puff Sts and next 2 chs, dc in next ch and in next 2 dc, skip next dc, work BPtr around next FPtr, dc in same FPtr just worked around and in next 9 dc †, skip next dc, work BPtr around next FPtr, ch 2, dc in next ch-3 sp, ch 4, skip next 2 Puff Sts and next 2 chs, dc in next ch, skip next dc, work BPtr around next FPtr, dc in same FPtr just worked around and in next 9 dc; repeat from ★ once **more**, then repeat from † to † once, hdc in next dc, work BPtr around same dc just worked into: 97 sts and 13 sps.

Row 11: Ch 3, turn; dc in next 12 sts, ★ † work FPtr around same BPtr just worked into, skip next dc, dc in next 2 dc and next 2 chs, ch 3, sc in next dc, ch 3, (dc, ch 2, dc) in next sc, ch 3, sc in next dc, ch 2, skip next dc, dc in next BPtr, work FPtr around same BPtr just worked into †, skip next dc, dc in next 10 sts, work FPtr around last st worked into, skip next dc, dc in next ch, ch 3, work (Puff St, ch 3) twice in next dc, dc in next BPtr, work FPtr around same BPtr just worked into, skip next dc, dc in next 10 sts; repeat from ★ once **more**, then repeat from † to † once, skip next dc, dc in next 7 dc, hdc in next dc, work FPtr around same dc just worked into: 107 sts and 21 sps.

Row 12: Ch 3, turn; dc in next 7 sts, ★ † skip next dc, work BPtr around next FPtr, dc in same FPtr just worked around and in next dc, ch 3, skip next 2 sps, work Puff St in next ch-2 sp, (ch 2, work Puff St in same sp) twice, ch 4, skip next sc and next 2 chs, dc in next ch and next 3 dc, skip next dc, work BPtr around next FPtr †, dc in same FPtr just worked around and in next 9 dc, skip next dc, work BPtr around next FPtr, ch 2, dc in next ch-3 sp, ch 4, skip next 2 Puff Sts and next 2 chs, dc in next ch, skip next dc, work BPtr around next FPtr, dc in same FPtr just worked around and in next 9 dc; repeat from ★ once **more**, then repeat from † to † once, dc in same FPtr just worked around and in next 11 dc, hdc in next dc, work BPtr around same dc just worked into: 103 sts and 14 sps.

Row 13: Ch 3, turn; dc in next 14 sts, ★ † work FPtr around same BPtr just worked into, skip next dc, dc in next 3 dc, ch 3, skip next ch-3 sp, work (Puff St, ch 2) twice in next ch-4 sp, work (Puff St, ch 2, Puff St) in next ch-2 sp, ch 3, dc in next 3 sts, work FPtr around last st worked into †, skip next dc, dc in next 10 sts, work FPtr around same BPtr just worked into, skip next dc, dc in next ch, ch 3, work (Puff St, ch 3) twice in next dc, dc in next BPtr, work FPtr around same BPtr just worked into, skip next dc, dc in next 10 sts; repeat from ★ once **more**, then repeat from † to † once, skip next dc, dc in next 5 dc, hdc in next dc, work FPtr around same dc just worked into: 110 sts and 21 sps.

Row 14: Ch 3, turn; dc in next 6 sts, ★ † work BPtr around next FPtr, dc in next 3 dc and next ch, ch 5, skip next 2 Puff Sts, sc in next ch-2 sp, ch 5, skip next 2 Puff Sts and next 2 chs, dc in next ch and next 3 dc, work BPtr around next FPtr †, dc in next 10 dc, work BPtr around next FPtr, dc in next dc, ch 2, skip next ch-3 sp, dc in next ch-3 sp, ch 3, dc in next dc, work BPtr around next FPtr, dc in next 10 dc; repeat from ★ once **more**, then repeat from † to † once, dc in next 13 dc, hdc in next dc, work BPtr around same dc just worked into: 105 sts and 10 sps.

Row 15: Ch 3, turn; dc in next 14 sts, ★ † work FPtr around next BPtr, dc in next 3 dc, ch 2, sc in next ch-5 sp, ch 3, (dc, ch 2, dc) in next sc, ch 3, sc in next ch-5 sp, ch 2, skip next dc, dc in next 3 dc, work FPtr around next BPtr †, dc in next 10 dc, work FPtr around next BPtr, dc in next dc, ch 2, work (Puff St, ch 3) twice in next dc, dc in next dc, work FPtr around next BPtr, dc in next 10 dc; repeat from ★ once **more**, then repeat from † to † once, dc in next 5 dc, hdc in next dc, work FPtr around same dc just worked into: 110 sts and 21 sps.

Row 16: Ch 3, turn; dc in next 6 sts, ★ † work BPtr around next FPtr, dc in next 3 dc, ch 3, skip next 2 sps, work Puff St in next ch-2 sp, (ch 2, work Puff St in same sp) twice, ch 4, skip next sc, dc in next 3 dc, work BPtr around next FPtr †, dc in next 10 dc, work BPtr around next FPtr, dc in next dc, ch 2, skip next ch-3 sp, dc in next ch-3 sp, ch 3, dc in next dc, work BPtr around next FPtr, dc in next 10 dc; repeat from ★ once **more**, then repeat from † to † once, dc in next 13 dc, hdc in next dc, work BPtr around same dc just worked into: 105 sts and 16 sps.

Row 17: Ch 3, turn; dc in next 14 sts, ★ † work FPtr around next BPtr, dc in next 3 dc, ch 3, skip next ch-4 sp, work (Puff St, ch 2) twice in next ch-2 sp, work (Puff St, ch 2, Puff St) in next ch-2 sp, ch 3, dc in next 3 dc, work FPtr around next BPtr †, dc in next 10 dc, work FPtr around next BPtr, dc in next dc, ch 3, work (Puff St, ch 3) twice in next dc, dc in next dc, work FPtr around next BPtr, dc in next 10 dc; repeat from ★ once **more**, then repeat from † to † once, dc in next 5 dc, hdc in next dc, work FPtr around same dc just worked into: 110 sts and 21 sps.

Row 18: Ch 3, turn; dc in next 7 sts, ★ † work BPtr around same FPtr just worked into, skip next dc, dc in next 2 dc and next ch, ch 4, skip next 2 Puff Sts, dc in next ch-2 sp, ch 4, skip next ch-2 sp, sc in next ch-3 sp, ch 4, skip next 2 dc, dc in next 2 sts, work BPtr around same FPtr just worked into, skip next dc †, dc in next 10 sts, work BPtr around same FPtr just worked into, skip next dc, dc in next ch, ch 4, skip next ch-3 sp, dc in next ch-3 sp, ch 2, skip next dc, work BPtr around next FPtr, skip next dc, dc in next 10 sts; repeat from ★ once **more**, then repeat from † to † once, dc in next 12 dc, hdc in next dc, work BPtr around same dc just worked into: 97 sts and 13 sps.

Row 19: Ch 3, turn; dc in next 12 sts, ★ † skip next dc, work FPtr around next BPtr, dc in same BPtr just worked around, ch 2, skip next dc, sc in next dc, ch 3, (dc, ch 2, dc) in next sc, ch 3, sc in next dc, ch 3, skip next 2 chs, dc in next 2 chs and in next 2 dc, skip next dc, work FPtr around next BPtr, dc in same BPtr just worked around †, dc in next 9 dc, skip next dc, work FPtr around next BPtr, dc in same BPtr just worked around, ch 3, work (Puff St, ch 3) twice in next dc, skip next 3 chs, dc in next ch, skip next dc, work FPtr around next BPtr, dc in same BPtr just worked around and in next 9 dc; repeat from ★ once **more**, then repeat from † to † once, dc in next 6 dc, hdc in next dc, work FPtr around same dc just worked into: 107 sts and 21 sps.

Row 20: Ch 3, turn; dc in next 9 sts, ★ † work BPtr around same FPtr just worked into, skip next dc, dc in next 3 dc and in next ch, ch 4, skip next ch-3 sp, work Puff St in next ch-2 sp, (ch 2, work Puff St in same sp) twice, ch 3, skip next 2 sps, dc in next 2 sts, work BPtr around same FPtr just worked into, skip next dc, dc in next 10 sts †, work BPtr around same FPtr just worked into, skip next dc, dc in next ch, ch 4, skip next ch-3 sp, dc in next ch-3 sp, ch 2, skip next dc, work BPtr around next FPtr, skip next dc, dc in next 10 sts; repeat from ★ once **more**, then repeat from † to † once, hdc in next dc, work BPtr around same dc just worked into: 103 sts and 16 sps.

Row 21: Ch 3, turn; dc in next 10 sts, ★ † skip next dc, work FPtr around next BPtr, dc in same BPtr just worked around and in next 2 dc, ch 3, skip next ch-3 sp, work (Puff St, ch 2) twice in next ch-2 sp, work (Puff St, ch 2, Puff St) in next ch-2 sp, ch 3, dc in next 3 dc, skip next dc, work FPtr around next BPtr, dc in same BPtr just worked around †, dc in next 9 dc, skip next dc, work FPtr around next BPtr, dc in same BPtr just worked around, ch 3, work (Puff St, ch 3) twice in next dc, skip next 3 chs, dc in next ch, skip next dc, work FPtr around next BPtr, dc in same BPtr just worked around and in next 9 dc; repeat from ★ once **more**, then repeat from † to † once, dc in next 8 dc, hdc in next dc, work FPtr around same dc just worked into: 110 sts and 21 sps.

Row 22: Ch 3, turn; dc in next 11 sts, ★ † work BPtr around same FPtr just worked into, skip next dc, dc in next 2 dc and next ch, ch 4, skip next 2 Puff Sts, dc in next ch-2 sp, ch 4, skip next ch-2 sp, sc in next ch-3 sp, ch 4, skip next 2 dc, dc in next 2 sts, work BPtr around same FPtr just worked into, skip next dc †, dc in next 10 sts, work BPtr around same FPtr just worked into, skip next dc, dc in next ch, ch 4, skip next ch-3 sp, dc in next ch-2 sp, ch 2, skip next dc, work BPtr around next FPtr, skip next dc, dc in next 10 sts; repeat from ★ once **more**, then repeat from † to † once, dc in next 8 dc, hdc in next dc, work BPtr around same dc just worked into: 97 sts and 13 sps.

Row 23: Ch 3, turn; dc in next 8 sts, ★ † skip next dc, work FPtr around next BPtr, dc in same BPtr just worked around, ch 2, skip next dc, sc in next dc, ch 3, (dc, ch 2, dc) in next sc, ch 3, sc in next dc, ch 3, skip next 2 chs, dc in next 2 chs and in next 2 dc, skip next dc, work FPtr around next BPtr, dc in same BPtr just worked around †, dc in next 9 dc, skip next dc, work FPtr around next BPtr, dc in same BPtr just worked around, ch 2, work (Puff St, ch 3) twice in next dc, skip next 3 chs, dc in next ch, skip next dc, work FPtr around next BPtr, dc in same BPtr just worked around and in next 9 dc; repeat from ★ once **more**, then repeat from † to † once, dc in next 10 dc, hdc in next dc, work FPtr around same dc just worked into: 107 sts and 21 sps.

Row 24: Ch 3, turn; dc in next 13 sts, ★ † work BPtr around same FPtr just worked into, skip next dc, dc in next 3 dc and in next ch, ch 4, skip next ch-3 sp, work Puff St in next ch-2 sp, (ch 2, work Puff St in same sp) twice, ch 3, skip next 2 sps, dc in next 2 sts, work BPtr around same FPtr just worked into, skip next dc †, dc in next 10 sts, work BPtr around same FPtr just worked into, skip next dc, dc in next ch, ch 4, skip next 2 Puff Sts, dc in next ch-3 sp, ch 2, skip next dc, work BPtr around next FPtr, skip next dc, dc in next 10 sts; repeat from ★ once **more**, then repeat from † to † once, dc in next 6 dc, hdc in next dc, work BPtr around same dc just worked into: 103 sts and 16 sps.

Row 25: Ch 3, turn; dc in next 6 sts, ★ † skip next dc, work FPtr around next BPtr, dc in same BPtr just worked around and in next 2 dc, ch 3, skip next ch-sp, work (Puff St, ch 2) twice in next ch-2 sp, work (Puff St, ch 2, Puff St) in next ch-2 sp, ch 3, dc in next 3 dc, skip next dc, work FPtr around next BPtr, dc in same BPtr just worked around †, dc in next 9 dc, skip next dc, work FPtr around next BPtr, dc in same BPtr just worked around, ch 3, work (Puff St, ch 3) twice in next dc, skip next 3 chs, dc in next ch, skip next dc, work FPtr around next BPtr, dc in same BPtr just worked around and in next 9 dc; repeat from ★ once **more**, then repeat from † to † once, dc in next 12 dc, hdc in next dc, work FPtr around same dc just worked into: 110 sts and 21 sps.

Row 26: Ch 3, turn; dc in next 14 sts, ★ † work BPtr around next FPtr, dc in next 3 dc and next ch, ch 5, skip next 2 Puff Sts, sc in next ch-2 sp, ch 5, skip next 2 Puff Sts and next 2 chs, dc in next ch and next 3 dc, work BPtr around next FPtr †, dc in next 10 dc, work BPtr around next FPtr, dc in next dc, ch 2, skip next sp, dc in next ch-3 sp, ch 3, dc in next dc, work BPtr around next FPtr, dc in next 10 dc; repeat from ★ once **more**, then repeat from † to † once, dc in next 5 dc, hdc in next dc, work BPtr around same dc just worked into: 105 sts and 10 sps.

Row 27: Ch 3, turn; dc in next 6 sts, ★ † work FPtr around next BPtr, dc in next 3 dc, ch 2, sc in next ch-5 sp, ch 3, (dc, ch 2, dc) in next sc, ch 3, sc in next ch-5 sp, ch 2, skip next dc, dc in next 3 dc, work FPtr around next BPtr †, dc in next 10 dc, work FPtr around next BPtr, dc in next dc, ch 3, work (Puff St, ch 3) twice in next dc, dc in next dc, work FPtr around next BPtr, dc in next 10 dc; repeat from ★ once **more**, then repeat from † to † once, dc in next 13 dc, hdc in next dc, work FPtr around same dc just worked into: 110 sts and 21 sps.

Rows 28-101: Repeat Rows 4-27, 3 times; then repeat Rows 4 and 5 once **more**.

Row 102: Ch 3, dc in next 14 sts, ★ † work BPtr around next FPtr, dc in next 3 dc and next ch, ch 5, skip next 2 Puff Sts, sc in next ch-2 sp, ch 5, skip next 2 Puff Sts and next 2 chs, dc in next ch and next 3 dc, work BPtr around next FPtr †, dc in next 10 dc, work BPtr around next FPtr, dc in next dc, ch 2, skip next ch-3 sp, sc in next ch-3 sp, ch 3, dc in next dc, work BPtr around next FPtr, dc in next 10 dc; repeat from ★ once **more**, then repeat from † to † once; dc in next 5 dc, hdc in next dc, work BPtr around same dc just worked into: 105 sts and 10 sps.

Row 103: Ch 3, dc in next 6 sts, ★ † work FPtr around next BPtr, dc in next 4 dc, 4 dc in next ch-5 sp, skip next sc, 4 dc in next ch-5 sp, dc in next 4 dc, work FPtr around next BPtr †, dc in next 10 dc, work FPtr around next BPtr, dc in next dc, 2 dc in next ch-3 sp, dc in next sc, 2 dc in next ch-2 sp, dc in next dc, work FPtr around next BPtr, dc in next 10 dc; repeat from ★ once **more**, then repeat from † to † once, dc in next 13 dc, hdc in next dc, work FPtr around same dc just worked into; finish off.

FRINGE

Using photo as a guide for placement and holding 10 strands of yarn together, each 16" (40.5 cm) long, add 17 fringe groups evenly spaced across each short edge of Afghan *(Fig. 6a & b, page 47)*.

GENERAL INSTRUCTIONS

ABBREVIATIONS

BPdtr	Back Post double treble crochet(s)
BPhdc	Back Post half double crochet(s)
BPtr	Back Post treble crochet(s)
BPtrtr	Back Post triple treble crochet(s)
BPtr2tog	Back Post treble crochet 2 together
ch(s)	chain(s)
cm	centimeters
dc	double crochet(s)
dc2tog	double crochet 2 together
dtr	double treble crochet(s)
FP	Front Post
FP2tog	Front Post 2 together
FPdtr	Front Post double treble crochet(s)
FPqtr	Front Post quadruple crochet(s)
FPtr	Front Post treble crochet(s)
FPtrtr	Front Post triple treble crochet(s)
hdc	half double crochet(s)
mm	millimeters
Rnd(s)	Round(s)
RS	right side
sc	single crochet(s)
sp(s)	space(s)
st(s)	stitch(es)
tr	treble crochet(s)
WS	wrong side
YO	yarn over

SYMBOLS & TERMS

★ — work instructions following ★ as many **more** times as indicated in addition to the first time.

† to † **or** ♥ to ♥ — work all instructions from first † to second † **or** first ♥ to second ♥ **as many** times as specified.

( ) or [ ] — work enclosed instructions **as many** times as specified by the number immediately following **or** work all enclosed instructions in the stitch or space indicated **or** contains explanatory remarks.

colon (:) — the number(s) given after a colon at the end of a row or round denote(s) the number of stitches or spaces you should have on that row or round.

CROCHET TERMINOLOGY		
UNITED STATES		INTERNATIONAL
slip stitch (slip st)	=	single crochet (sc)
single crochet (sc)	=	double crochet (dc)
half double crochet (hdc)	=	half treble crochet (htr)
double crochet (dc)	=	treble crochet (tr)
treble crochet (tr)	=	double treble crochet (dtr)
double treble crochet (dtr)	=	triple treble crochet (ttr)
triple treble crochet (tr tr)	=	quadruple treble crochet (qtr)
skip	=	miss

BEGINNER	Projects for first-time crocheters using basic stitches. Minimal shaping.
EASY	Projects using yarn with basic stitches, repetitive stitch patterns, simple color changes, and simple shaping and finishing.
INTERMEDIATE	Projects using a variety of techniques, such as basic lace patterns or color patterns, mid-level shaping and finishing.
EXPERIENCED	Projects with intricate stitch patterns, techniques and dimension, such as non-repeating patterns, multi-color techniques, fine threads, small hooks, detailed shaping and refined finishing.

CROCHET HOOKS																	
U.S.	B-1	C-2	D-3	E-4	F-5	G-6	7	H-8	I-9	J-10	K-10½	L-11	M/N-13	N/P-15	P/Q	Q	S
Metric - mm	2.25	2.75	3.25	3.5	3.75	4	4.5	5	5.5	6	6.5	8	9	10	15	16	19

GAUGE

Exact gauge is **essential** for proper size. Before beginning your project, make the sample swatch given in the individual instructions in the yarn and hook specified. After completing the swatch, measure it, counting your stitches and rows carefully. If your swatch is larger or smaller than specified, **make another, changing hook size to get the correct gauge**. Keep trying until you find the size hook that will give you the specified gauge.

JOINING WITH SC

When instructed to join with sc, begin with a slip knot on hook. Insert hook in stitch or space indicated, YO and pull up a loop, YO and draw through both loops on hook.

JOINING WITH DC

When instructed to join with dc, begin with a slip knot on hook. YO, holding loop on hook, insert hook in stitch or space indicated, YO and pull up a loop (3 loops on hook), (YO and draw through 2 loops on hook) twice.

BACK OR FRONT LOOP ONLY

Work only in loop(s) indicated by arrow ***(Fig. 1)***.

Fig. 1

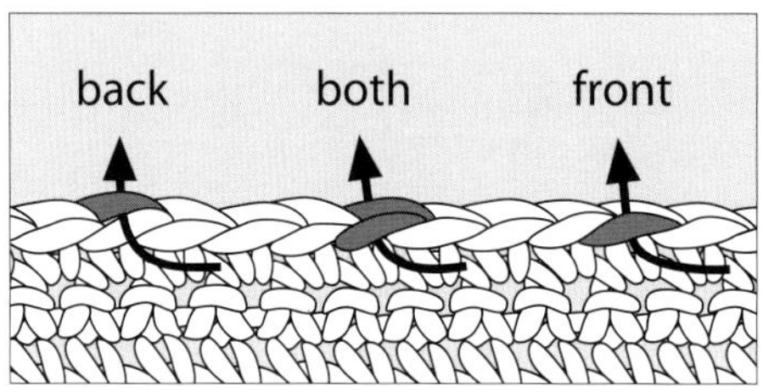

FREE LOOPS

After working in Back or Front Loops Only on a row or round, there will be a ridge of unused loops. These are called the free loops. Later, when instructed to work in the free loops of the same row or round, work in these loops ***(Fig. 2a)***.

When instructed to work in free loops of a chain, work in loop indicated by arrow ***(Fig. 2b)***.

Fig. 2a

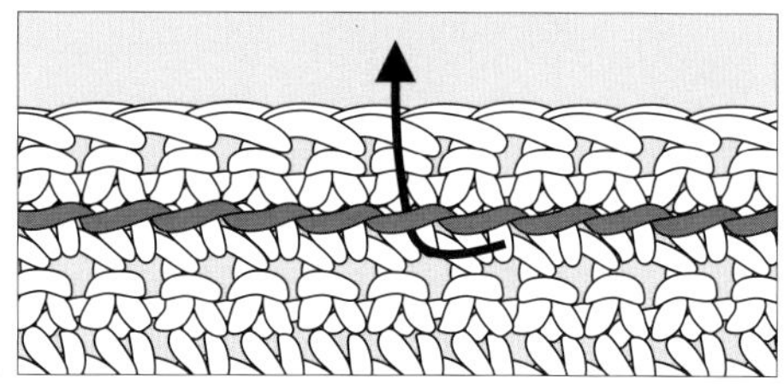

Fig. 2b

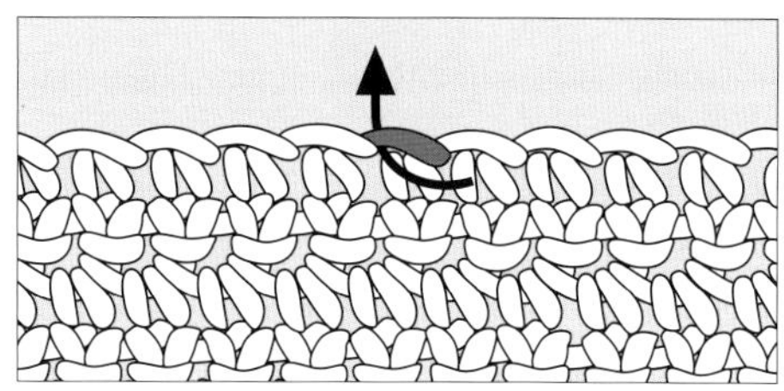

Yarn Weight Symbol & Names	LACE 0	SUPER FINE 1	FINE 2	LIGHT 3	MEDIUM 4	BULKY 5	SUPER BULKY 6	JUMBO 7
Type of Yarns in Category	Fingering, size 10 crochet thread	Sock, Fingering, Baby	Sport, Baby	DK, Light Worsted	Worsted, Afghan, Aran	Chunky, Craft, Rug	Super Bulky, Roving	Jumbo, Roving
Crochet Gauge* Ranges in Single Crochet to 4" (10 cm)	32-42 sts**	21-32 sts	16-20 sts	12-17 sts	11-14 sts	8-11 sts	6-9 sts	5 sts and fewer
Advised Hook Size Range	Steel*** 6 to 8, Regular hook B-1	B-1 to E-4	E-4 to 7	7 to I-9	I-9 to K-10½	K-10½ to M/N-13	M/N-13 to Q	Q and larger

*GUIDELINES ONLY: The chart above reflects the most commonly used gauges and hook sizes for specific yarn categories.

** Lace weight yarns are usually crocheted with larger hooks to create lacy openwork patterns. Accordingly, a gauge range is difficult to determine. Always follow the gauge stated in your pattern.

*** Steel crochet hooks are sized differently from regular hooks–the higher the number, the smaller the hook, which is the reverse of regular hook sizing.

POST STITCH

Work around post of stitch indicated, inserting hook in direction of arrow *(Fig. 3)*.

Fig. 3

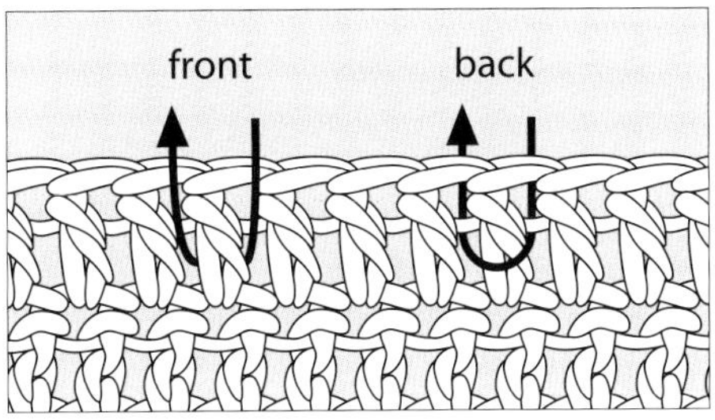

SIDE TWO LEGS OF A STITCH

When instructed to work in **side** two legs of a stitch, insert hook under two loops at base of stitch in direction of arrow *(Fig. 4)*.

Fig. 4

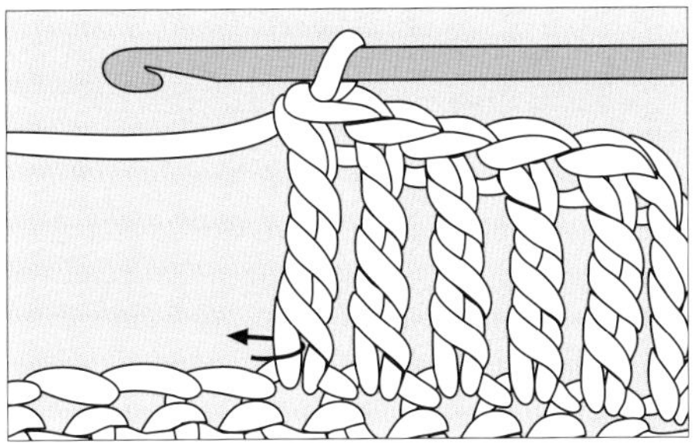

REVERSE SINGLE CROCHET

(abbreviated reverse sc)

Working from **left** to **right**, ★ insert hook in stitch to right of hook ***(Fig. 5a)***, YO and draw through, under and to left of loop on hook (2 loops on hook) ***(Fig. 5b)***, YO and draw through both loops on hook ***(Fig. 5c)*** **(reverse sc made, *Fig. 5d*)**; repeat from ★ across.

Fig. 5a

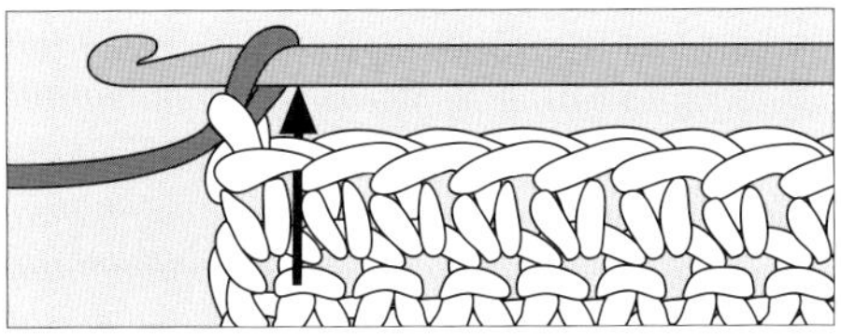

Fig. 5b

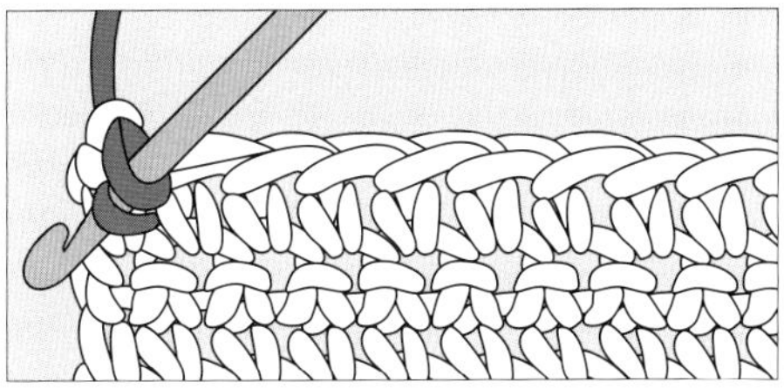

Fig. 5c

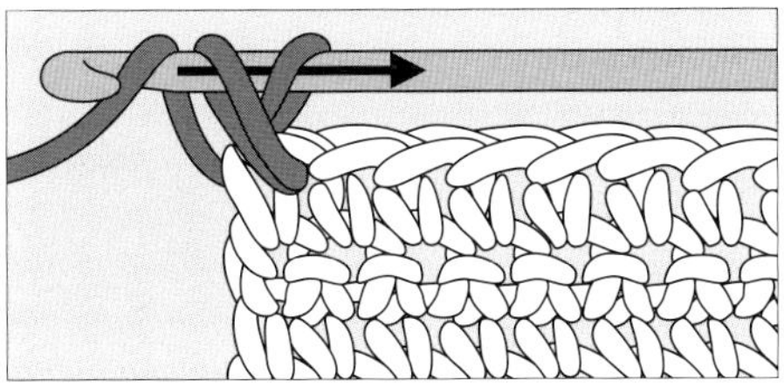

Fig. 5d

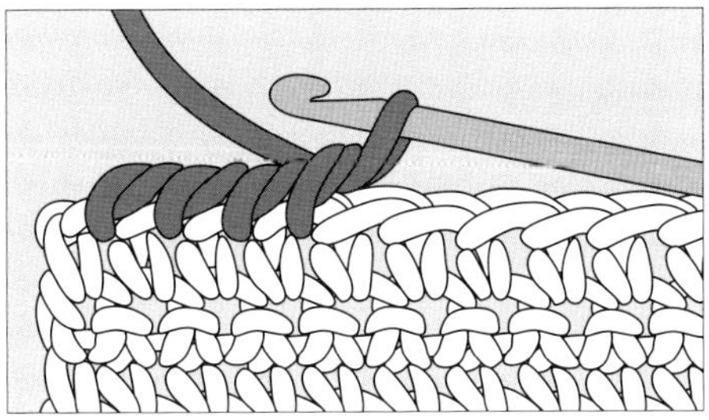

FRINGE

Cut a piece of cardboard 5" (12.5 cm) wide and and half as long as strands indicated in individual instructions. Wind the yarn **loosely** and **evenly** lengthwise around the cardboard until the card is filled, then cut across one end; repeat as needed.

Hold together as many strands as specified in individual instructions; fold in half.

With **wrong** side facing and using a crochet hook, draw the folded end up through a stitch and pull the loose ends through the folded end *(Fig. 6a)*; draw the knot up **tightly** *(Fig. 6b)*. Repeat, spacing as specified in individual instructions.

Lay flat on a hard surface and trim the ends.

Fig. 6a

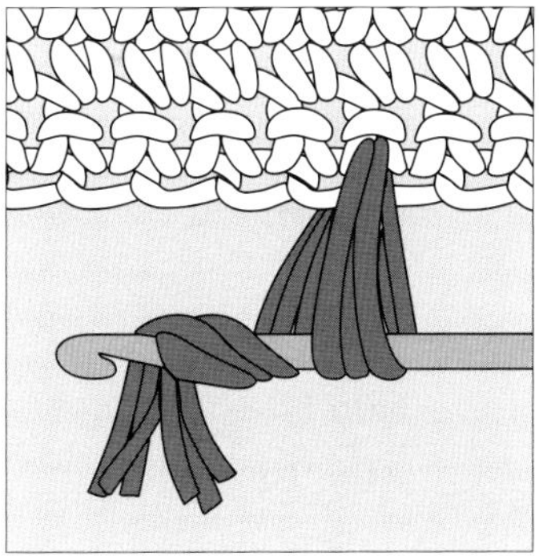

Fig. 6b

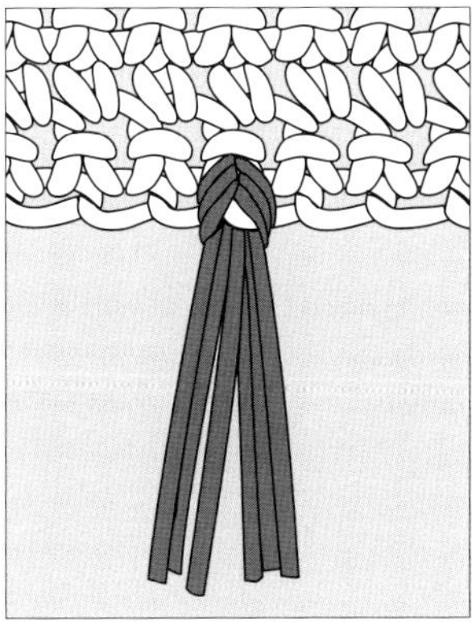

YARN INFORMATION

Each afghan in this book was made using Medium Weight Yarn. Any brand of Medium Weight Yarn may be used. It is best to refer to the yardage/meters when determining how many balls or skeins to purchase. Remember, to arrive at the finished size, it is the GAUGE/TENSION that is important, not the brand of yarn.

For your convenience, listed below are the specific yarns used to create our photography models. Because yarn manufacturers make frequent changes to their product lines, you may sometimes find it necessary to use a substitute yarn or to search for the discontinued product at alternate suppliers (locally or online).

SHELL GALLERY
Caron® Simply Soft®
#9755 Sunshine

GIRLIE FISHERMAN
Lion Brand® Vanna's Choice®
#101 Pink

TRIANGLES
Patons® Canadiana™
#10747 Teal Heather

MOSTLY POSTS
Caron® Simple Soft® Heathers™
#9509 Grey Heather

VIGNETTES
Patons® Classic Wool Worsted™
#77742 Gingerbread

A SHOWER OF LEAVES
Lion Brand® Heartland®
#173 Everglades

FLORAL CAMEOS
Lion Brand® Jeans®
#109W Stonewash

WINDING PATHS
Patons® Canadiana™
#10012 Toasty Grey

We have made every effort to ensure that these instructions are accurate and complete. We cannot, however, be responsible for human error, typographical mistakes, or variations in individual work.

Production Team: Instructional/ Technical Editor - Sarah J. Green; Editorial Writer - Susan Frantz Wiles; Senior Graphic Artist - Lora Puls; Graphic Artist - Victoria Temple; Photo Stylist - Lori Wenger; and Photographer - Jason Masters.

Made In U.S.A.

Meet Rena V. Stevens

Designing knit and crochet has always been both her driving passion and her comfort zone in life, says Rena V. Stevens.

The actual crocheting of the design is her favorite part of the process. "It's like working on a fun puzzle, with a satisfying and lasting prize at the end," she says.

She learned needle arts during elementary school in the Netherlands and continued working with it throughout her childhood in Canada and California. Later, her career as a community college teacher of business courses allowed her to do lots of designing during summer vacations and other breaks.

"Now retired, I stay busier than ever with a husband, dog, cat, new house, and babysitting our grandson for our daughter and son-in-law, both veterinarians with long, sometimes unpredictable working hours," she says.